THE
Archive Photographs
SERIES

MARYLEBONE

The Crawford Street Fire from Seymour Buildings, Seymour Place, 16 August 1914. This disaster destroyed the premises of motor and coach builders Philip Fairbridge & Son, together with fifty-six cars and carriages left there for repairs. Residential Tarrant Place stands here now, beside St Mary's church, Wyndham Place, whose tower can be seen above the ruins.

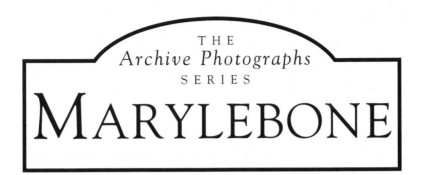

THE
Archive Photographs
SERIES
MARYLEBONE

Compiled by
Brian Girling

CHALFORD

First published 1997
Copyright © Brian Girling, 1997

The Chalford Publishing Company
St Mary's Mill, Chalford,
Stroud, Gloucestershire, GL6 8NX

ISBN 0 7524 1014 8

Typesetting and origination by
The Chalford Publishing Company
Printed in Great Britain by
Bailey Print, Dursley, Gloucestershire

Eggs were 1/- per dozen at Andrew Dilling's Devonshire Dairy around 1905. The site between Nottingham Street and Northumberland Street (Luxborough Street) was covered by the Marylebone telephone exchange during the 1920s.

Contents

London Street Musicians.

Riding House Street, *c.* 1904. Some Marylebone street life of yesteryear, as itinerant musicians entertain a group of local children beside Gustave Lyon's Hairdressing Salon, Dr George Jackson's surgery and the Star Coffee House.

Acknowledgements

A book like this is the richer for the contributions and help of others and I would particularly like to thank Tony Davies of Marylebone Gallery; London Metropolitan Archives; David Brewster and Micky Shephard. A special 'thank you' is due to the staff at the Westminster Archives Centre for their unfailing helpfulness.

Introduction

Marylebone was one of London's smaller metropolitan boroughs until 1965, when amalgamation with neighbouring Westminster and Paddington created a newer, larger City of Westminster. Contained within the boundaries of the original borough are some of London's most popular attractions linked by streets containing numerous late Georgian town houses, all helping to maintain the special appeal of this highly individual quarter of London. Marylebone is home to such diverse institutions as Lord's Cricket Ground, the London Zoo, Madame Tussaud's, the London Planetarium and the BBC. Marble Arch is at Marylebone's south-western corner, while Regent's Park occupies a large part of the borough's acreage further north.

Oxford Street, Europe's premier shopping street, forms Marylebone's southern boundary and the private medical profession is famously ensconced behind the hallowed portals of Harley Street and Wimpole Street. Famous people have long been attracted to Marylebone's spacious houses and central location, including Lord Byron, who lived in Holles Street; Charles Dickens, who was a resident of Devonshire Terrace and Sheridan, who wrote *The Duenna* and *The Rivals* at his home in Orchard Street. In fiction, Sir Arthur Conan Doyle's Sherlock Holmes and Dr Watson operated from their lodgings in Baker Street, where a convenient hansom would always be on hand to convey the pair about the labyrinthine fog-shrouded metropolis.

The history of what we now know as Marylebone began when the Romans built roads from their settlement of Londinium (London) towards the west and north-west of the country. These roads are still in evidence; we know them as Edgware Road and Oxford Street, but in Roman times, the town was far away behind its protecting walls.

At the time of the Norman Conquest, the area beside the Roman roads consisted of two manors: Tyburn, by what would later become Oxford Street and Lilestone (Lisson), close to Watling Street, or the Edgware Road.

The village of Tyburn slowly evolved beside the waters of the Tyburn brook and its ancient church of St John was replaced by a new building upstream, which was dedicated to St Mary. This settlement became known as St Mary by the Brook, or Bourne, then St Mary Le Bourne and then St Marylebone. The name Tyburn gradually lost favour due to the notoriety surrounding its infamous gallows, which stood by what is now Marble Arch.

By the eighteenth century, great changes were at hand for the picturesque place which Londoners loved to visit for its healthy air, rustic surroundings and the pleasure grounds of Marylebone Gardens, which had been laid out behind Marylebone's manor house from 1650. The streets of Soho and fashionable Mayfair began to be matched on the north side of Tyburn

Road (Oxford Street), first by the splendours of Cavendish Square, and then by rows of flat-fronted town houses which gradually spread northwards across the fields. The houses catered for all classes, with lordly Portman Square at one end of the social scale and the overcrowded tenements and cottages of Lisson Grove at the other. Further out, leafy St John's Wood became fashionable with its pretty houses and classical villas and Regent's Park, bordered by its breathtaking Regency terraces was a creation of the early nineteenth century. Portland Town was once a slummy quarter beyond Regent's Park until it was gentrified into St John's Wood's smart shopping centre.

The advent of the railways, two world wars and a host of redevelopments have changed the face of parts of Marylebone many times. This book takes us on a tour of the old borough and looks at its streets, characters and shops as they were around the early part of this century. Many scenes have survived the century well and will look familiar, while others have long passed into distant memory, which it is hoped may be revived by these historic images.

Photographic reproductions of many of the photographs are available from the author at 17 Devonshire Road, Harrow, HA1 4LS.

Gosfield Street and Langham works, c. 1910.

One
Oxford Street

Oxford Street, c. 1920. Oxford Street's fame as a shopping street is worldwide, its straightness throughout a length of over a mile from Marble Arch to St Giles Circus a legacy of its Roman origins when it was known as the 'Via Trinobantia'. The road has been at various times in its history known as 'The King's Highway', 'Tyburn (or Tibourne) Way', and 'The Road to Oxford', but the name Oxford Street was adopted during the eighteenth century, when land on the north side was acquired by Edward Harley, second earl of Oxford. Housing development began around 1739, but it was not until the nineteenth century that Oxford Street began to lose its residential character as a host of small shops began to replace the houses and inns, with the department stores for which the street is renowned arriving around the 1860s. The view typifies the enduring popularity of this, the ultimate shopping street, with lively traffic and crowded pavements beside the store of one of the great names of Oxford Street: Peter Robinson. That store was rebuilt in 1924 in the solid, stone-fronted style of the '20s. Further along, the Edwardian emporium of house furnishers Waring & Gillow can be seen rising above its older neighbours. Oxford Street was, until 1965, the boundary between Marylebone and the City of Westminster. The terra-cotta frontage of Oxford Circus station, which opened on 30 July 1900, can be seen on the right.

Marble Arch, *c*. 1909. This notable London landmark of Italian marble at the western end of Oxford Street was designed by John Nash and erected in front of Buckingham Palace in 1830 prior to removal to its present position in 1851. For over fifty years, Marble Arch formed part of the Cumberland Gate to Hyde Park before increasing traffic congestion early in the twentieth century necessitated the setting back of the gates further into Hyde Park, leaving Marble Arch isolated in the middle of the road, as we see it here. The site of Tyburn, London's principal place of public execution from the fourteenth to the eighteenth century, is to the left of the view.

Oxford Street from Marble Arch, c. 1903. Less than a century has seen this view change beyond all recognition, with the modern buildings of the new Oxford Street replacing their more modest predecessors. These included a branch of Express Dairies, left, with the Victorian gentility of a 'ladies tea room' on the first floor behind a sunny balcony overlooking Park Lane and Hyde Park.

Marble Arch station, *c*. 1903. The revolutionary deep level electric tube, the Central London Railway (Central Line), opened on 30 July 1900, its original route running from Shepherd's Bush to the City of London. The new railway proved extremely popular, the clean efficiency of its electric traction contrasting with the vaporous exhalations experienced on London's older steam driven railways. A flat fare of 2d soon earned the line the nickname 'Tuppeny Tube'. The former entrance to the station on the Old Quebec Street corner is seen here, while the City of Quebec pub, whose landlord was George Shepherd, stood on the nearer corner. John Baker's hairdressing salon was next door and on the right, the Star Photographic Co. ('Millions of smiles, we are absolutely the best'), had an 'artistic studio' where cabinet photographs and *cartes-de-visite* could be obtained. The Mount Royal Hotel was built on the sites of these shops in 1934.

The Church of the Annunciation, Old Quebec Street from Marble Arch, *c.* 1929. The demolition of houses and shops seen in the preceding photographs opened up a rare view of this distinctive church, built between 1912/4 to the designs of Sir Walter Tapper. Marble Arch station, right, had, by this time, been surmounted by the short-lived Marble Arch Hotel. Work began on a new station entrance in 1930, which opened on 15 August 1932, with the new Cumberland Hotel eventually taking over the whole block from Old Quebec Street to Great Cumberland Place.

Oxford Street from Marble Arch, *c.* 1906. The western entrance to Oxford Street was modest indeed, with humble mews houses on the Park Lane corner, right, where Hereford House now stands. To the left, the single storey Marble Arch station was awaiting the hotel which would soon be built above it.

Oxford Street, c. 1912. These were typical of the small shops that formerly existed at the western end of Oxford Street. In the midst of them was one of the West End's earliest cinemas, the Electric Palace, which opened on 9 November 1908 with seating for 588 people. A tea room in the Japanese style was added in 1909 and the cinema lasted until 1933, when, together with the rest of the terrace, it was demolished to be replaced by the Mount Royal Hotel. The narrow frontage of the old cinema is easily spotted with its bright paint and tall flagpole.

The Mount Royal Hotel, c. 1935. The Mount Royal Hotel brought the sleek, streamlined style of the 1930s to Oxford Street, together with the usual row of shops on the ground floor. Only one of these had opened for business when photographed: a Dolcis shoe shop with the latest neon lettering adorning its frontage. Old Quebec Street is on the left.

Oxford Street by Hereford Gardens, *c*. 1900. Oxford Street could still show some welcome greenery early in the century, to contrast with the continuous rows of shops, but this vanished when British Industries House was built on the site of Hereford Gardens in 1931. A Gamage's store took the retail floors, but this was an unsuccessful venture and closure was followed by the opening of a branch of C & A Modes, which is still there. Road works (see next page) had caused these unusually traffic free conditions.

Oxford Street by Hereford Gardens, *c*. 1907. This was the long terrace of small shops between Old Quebec Street and Portman Street before their replacement in 1934 by the Mount Royal Hotel. This postcard view was sent to a lady in New York by a visitor to London who had apparently enjoyed a ride on the top deck of one of London's horse-buses, apart from 'going up and down the stairs'.

Oxford Street from Portman Street, *c.* 1900. This photograph further illustrates the modest nature of the shops at the western end of Oxford Street before the great department stores became established. Here we see part of a long-vanished pub, the Delaware Arms, on the Portman Street corner, left, with Louis Taddei's confectionary shop next door. H.J. Bound Ltd., the drapers, then occupied a couple of shops further along the street. The closed shutters suggest this was a Sunday afternoon and the total absence of traffic in this, the busiest of thoroughfares, is indeed a rare sight. This was due, however, to the road works which were giving Oxford Street a new wood block road surface. Note the long walls of wooden paving blocks along the kerb-side, stacked ready to be laid on the carriageway. Wooden paving was once commonplace in London and an experimental version of it was tried in Oxford Street (near Tottenham Court Road) as early as 1839, but it was not a success and was replaced by granite setts in 1844. Residential property still stood on the south (right) side of the road, but was swept away in favour of the concrete horrors of the 1960s.

Orchard Street to Duke Street, *c.* 1902. A ragged collection of small shops and the odd pub made up a particularly long terrace, but this block was destined for greatness and would soon accommodate one of the most spectacular of London's retailing emporia: Selfridges. American entrepreneur Harry Gordon Selfridge arrived in London from Chicago in 1906 with the intention of founding 'a department store, the like of which London had not seen before' and this Oxford Street location was selected by him as being ideal for his purpose. The long unbroken frontage on to London's premier shopping street allowed plenty of room for future expansion. Besides the numerous small shops, some larger businesses were already here, including the furniture shop of Sam Gillow of Waring & Gillow fame and a branch of drapers Lloyd & Co., located in four shops by Orchard Street, left.

Oxford Street by Orchard Street, *c.* 1907. By 1907, Lloyd & Co. had themselves expanded beyond their four shops into Orchard Street and other shops along the future Selfridge frontage. As may be seen, Lloyd's had tidied up and unified their upper floors since the earlier view above.

Selfridges, July 1919. A similar viewpoint to that of the photograph at the top of the preceding page reveals the first part of the great Selfridge building which would, in time, occupy the whole of this long frontage. The foundation stone was laid by H.G. Selfridge in 1908 and the first part of the store, at the Duke Street end of the block, was ready for opening day in March 1909. The old Lloyd's premises were acquired by Selfridge in 1914, who, as we can see here, occupied them with further departments until rebuilding could be completed. Selfridges also acquired a block of shops on the opposite (south) side of the road. The photograph records a time of jubilation in London, with parades and decorated streets in honour of the peace which at last had ended the weary years of the First World War. H.G. Selfridge, ever the showman, erected a series of huge plaster monuments and other patriotic displays along both sides of Oxford Street, beginning the store's long tradition of lavish decoration at times of national celebration. The road traffic in 1919 was an equal mixture of horse drawn and motorised. Remarkably, the advertisements on the buses all promote products that are still with us: Heinz Baked Beans, Pears Soap and Schweppes Ginger Ale.

Selfridges from Granville Place, *c*. 1925. H.G. Selfridge was always ready to espouse the latest electronic wonders of his age: the new wireless service being a typical example. In April 1925, the British Broadcasting Company, whose call sign was 2LO, began transmitting from two 150 feet high lattice masts on Selfridges roof, which continued to function until October 1929. Meanwhile, an early form of television was demonstrated in the store during the 1920s by its inventor, John Logie Baird. The view is of the back of the store looking towards Somerset Street, which was closed and built over by a still expanding Selfridges in the mid 1950s. The further part of Granville Place also disappeared during an expansion of the neighbouring Marks & Spencer.

The Silver Jubilee, May 1935. Bunting and flags filled the streets of London as the nation celebrated the Silver Jubilee of King George V and Queen Mary. Selfridges is just visible through the displays with, to the left of it, by Orchard Street, the new Marks & Spencer's store which had been erected five years previously.

Coronation Decorations, Selfridges, May 1937. The death of King George V came only seven months after his Jubilee and following the drama of the abdication of his successor, King Edward VIII, in 1936, it was time for national rejoicing once more with the Coronation on 12 May 1937 of King George VI and Queen Elizabeth (the Queen Mother). As usual, Selfridges celebrated with lavish decoration, which included a series of reliefs depicting scenes from English history running along the length of the frontage. Those nearest the camera portrayed the druids at Stonehenge, Queen Boudicea in her chariot and the Roman occupation of Britain.

Selfridges, c. 1935. The year 1927 saw the completion of the noble Selfridge facade. The last section to be finished was the main entrance at the centre, above which stands the great statue, the Queen of Time, incorporating the famous chiming clock. Among the numerous attractions of the store were a roof-top ice rink and a roof garden, the 'Hanging Gardens of Selfridges', where mannequin parades once took place.

Oxford Street from Stratford Place, c. 1933. Stratford Place, left, is a pleasant cul-de-sac of eighteenth century origin, with a fine stone-fronted mansion, Derby House, now the home of the Oriental Club. To the right, the His Masters Voice store is still here, but in premises rebuilt in 1938/9. At Doral's beauty parlour next door, a lady could obtain a permanent wave for 10/- 'for the whole head, no extras'. A slight dip in the roadway nearby was part of the shallow valley of the Tyburn brook, which once flowed through open fields, before it was culverted as the area became built up. Oxford Street's traffic remains dominated by its many bus routes, but cars are now officially excluded.

Sandwich man, Oxford Street, *c.* 1924. This gentleman, a member of a once prolific London tribe, carries a sandwich-board advertising another of Oxford Street's hairdressers, Maison Cavendish at number 327. In this earlier view, the 'perm' cost a mere 2/-, with the assurance that there would be 'no frizz', while 'shingling' refers to the fashionable short haircut of the day.

St Christophers Place, *c*. 1924. Oxford Street has many side turnings, where smaller specialist shops offer an alternative to the grand displays of the main road. At the beginning of the twentieth century, St Christophers Place was remarkable for the number of small furniture dealers trading here and, as the decades passed, it became a favourite with the antiques trade. It is now home to a variety of small exlusive shops, but this one, Jac's, specialists in artificial flowers, has been replaced by a smart modern restaurant.

Barrett Street and St Christophers Place, *c*. 1955. Although most of these buildings still stand, the work-a-day fifties gloom has been swept away and the area transformed into a delightful pedestrian precinct, with trees, flower baskets, a water feature, ornamental seats and attractive pavement cafes. Even the public loo has been prettified with greenery and intricate ironwork. The view recalls some familiar sights from the recent past, including a Lyons delivery van and a branch of MacFisheries on the James Street corner.

Oxford Street by New Bond Street, *c.* 1908. The Victorian buildings which housed D.H. Evans, the drapers, are seen beside Chapel Place, right, while a more distant row of sunblinds highlight the premises of another great department store, Marshall & Snelgrove, the silk mercers. On the opposite (Westminster) side of the road, some very modest property then occupied the corners of New Bond Street. Further along, a tall building of 1905 vintage housed the International Aspirator Company, purveyors of that housewives boon, the 'Aspirator Vacuum Cleaning Machine'.

Marshall & Snelgrove, *c.* 1904. The store was founded in 1837 at 11 Vere Street and by 1870 had expanded into these handsome premises between Vere Street and Marylebone Lane. The sender of this postcard in 1904 was most impressed with it all, writing 'Wish you could have seen Marshall & Snelgrove's on Thursday, it was decorated beautifully for the King and Queen of Portugal - we had a grand view'. Lively activity in the street included the usual jay-walkers, white-coated orderly boys with scoops (for the horse droppings), a postman with an empty sack and a 'growler' (a four-wheeled cab) awaiting a fare on its rank where there was 'standing for six Hackney carriages'.

Chapel Place, Oxford Street, *c.* 1903. Chapel Place is another of Oxford Street's side turnings, but there was only one shop here, that of Misses M. and F. Holmes, stationers and newsagents. This little family business lay in the shadow of the famous D.H. Evans department store, whose expansions in 1909 and 1937 swallowed up the sites of the Holmes' shop and Chapel Place Mansions which lay beyond it.

Oxford Street by Holles Street, c. 1905. Oxford Street's parade of vast department stores continued with the premises of another of its most famous names: John Lewis. The shop's beginnings in 1864 at a single Oxford Street store were modest; indeed the first days takings were apparently less than £1. Succeeding decades of prosperity led to increasing expansion, with the store eventually occupying blocks to the east and west of Holles Street.

Oxford Street by Holles Street, 18 September 1940. The buildings in the preceding photograph are seen again, this time in the early morning sunshine following their spectacular destruction by fire during a night-time air raid, when John Lewis' was struck by a pair of High Explosive bombs.

Holles Street, 18 September 1940. The scale of the damage wrought upon John Lewis' can be seen more easily here and shows how the intensity of the fire caused much of the building to collapse into Holles Street. Lord Byron, the poet, was born at number 24 Holles Street in a much more peaceful year, 1788.

John Lewis' Store, early 1940s. The dangerously damaged upper floors had been cleared away, leaving only wrecked ground floor shops facing on to Oxford Street, while a board directed shoppers towards Lewis' eastern block, where trading was still in progress. Later on, these single-storey remains were adapted as temporary shops, pending the store's complete rebuilding. Exhibitions of war-time industry were held by the government during the Second World War on part of John Lewis' bomb damaged site. The fine, modern, John Lewis' we see today dates from 1958/60.

T.G. Harries and Co., *c.* 1906. Despite an impressive frontage onto Oxford Street, broken only by the narrow entrance to long vanished Phoenix Yard, the drapery store of Thomas Jones Harries & Co. did not survive beyond 1928, when it was taken over by neighbouring John Lewis', who used the buildings to establish their eastern block of departments. The site is now covered by a vast building of 1957/62 vintage, with a branch of British Home Stores, a host of smaller shops, and the London College of Fashion on the floors above them.

Oxford Circus, *c*. 1905. Oxford Circus, or Regent Circus North, as it was originally known, was created as part of John Nash's visionary Regent Street scheme, which gave London a grand new thoroughfare running from Marylebone Park (Regent's Park), to Carlton House, Pall Mall, the palace of the Prince Regent. The new road opened in 1820 and soon became a street of fashionable shops, which spilled out into what was then a partly residential Oxford Street. Regent Street's other major junction was Regent Circus South, which was similar in shape and size to Oxford Circus when first built, before later enlargement led to its transformation into a much more famous place: Piccadilly Circus. Our early Edwardian view has captured Oxford Circus at a time when its elegant Nash buildings were still standing and looks into the eastern part of Oxford Street revealing yet another of the street's celebrated emporia, that of Peter Robinson. This is another company which began as a small outlet when the founder set up as a linen draper at 103 Oxford Street, went on to acquire five adjacent shops from 1854 to 1860 and susequently further properties in Oxford Street and Regent Street. The buildings we see here were replaced in 1924 by an imposing new store, built in the more grandiose stone-fronted style of the twentieth century. Here, a sunny summers day has brought the shoppers out and there is the usual array of horse-drawn public transport including a Hansom cab, whose quilted upholstery recalls a degree of comfort long vanished from London's streets.

Regent Street from Oxford Circus, *c*. 1904. A wet day in town has not emptied the pavements and the passengers on the top deck of a one penny horse-bus to Charing Cross brave the elements beneath a large umbrella. In the distance, the outline of Regent House is visible through the murk. Built in 1899, it was the first of the new stone-fronted buildings of Regent Street to replace the old Nash terraces.

Cockney Flower Girls, Oxford Circus, *c*. 1912. Piccadilly Circus and Oxford Circus were favourite sales pitches for these ladies with their baskets and pails piled high with blooms. The view looks north towards All Souls Church and Langham Place (see also p. 106).

Oxford Street from Oxford Circus, *c.* 1905. The view highlights some of the fancy ironwork which adorned Peter Robinson's frontage, while on the other side of the road by Argyll Street, a building site had work in progress on the Oxford Circus station of the Baker Street and Waterloo Railway (Bakerloo line). This would open on 10 March 1906 and join the Central London Railway station on the opposite corner, which had opened in 1900. There would be a new underground concourse linking the two stations from 1914.

Oxford Circus, *c.* 1931. By this time, the rebuilding of Regent Street in a grander style had swept away the last of Nash's Regency buildings and given Oxford Circus the stone-fronted structures we know today. The once separate Oxford Circus stations are visible here, while some of the older buses still have outmoded exterior staircases, the last relics of the days when all buses had open top decks.

Oxford Street, May 1903. Franco-British fervour filled the West End streets with flags and colourful decorations for the visit of the President of France during May 1903. Meanwhile, another great palace of retailing, Waring & Gillow, the house furnishers, rises behind temporary structures and covered pavements in front of its building site. Construction began in 1901 and the store opened in 1906. Two of Oxford Street's long vanished theatres are just visible here: the Princess's Theatre by Winsley Street, which opend in 1836 and was named in honour of Princess (later Queen) Victoria and the former Pantheon, which dated back to 1773. The Pantheon closed in 1867 and is seen here behind a mass of flags (centre), in the days when it was a wine store for Gilbey's. A Marks & Spencer store arose on the site in 1937.

Oxford Street, c. 1908. The completed Waring & Gillows, its architecture described by Sir Nikolaus Pevsner as 'riotous Hampton Court Baroque', is on the right, while further along, a roof-top flagpole marks the presence of the Peter Robinson store. A small curiosity of Oxford Street is that, with the exception of C & A's at Marble Arch, all the major department stores are on the sunny, south-facing Marylebone side of the street.

London Piano & Radio Ltd., 243 Oxford Street, c. 1938. In addition to its celebrated department stores, Oxford Street had its fair share of smaller specialist shops, including this one, where a new electronic wonder was available for those who could afford it: television. Beginning on 2 November 1936, the first television programmes were broadcast from North London's Alexandra Palace for a mere two hours a day and television sets or 'televisors' as they were then called, cost nearly as much as a new car. A televisor on show here was priced at 85 guineas.

Frascati's, Oxford Street, c. 1907. The roadway at this, the eastern end of Oxford Street, was narrower and the shops smaller and rather less fashionable, but in their midst and behind an unassuming fascade, right, a most opulent establishment could be found - Frascati's Restaurant. It was built in 1893 and featured a spectacular winter garden restaurant, which was lavishly enhanced with tropical greenery, all beneath a glass roof. A building which dates from the mid-1950s stands here now.

The Oxford Music Hall, c. 1908. The eastern end of Oxford Street forms the northern boundary of London's theatreland, but in a street which is totally dedicated to the shopper, there are few reminders of a theatrical past. The Oxford opened on the site of an old inn, the Boar & Castle, in 1861 and after a series of fires and rebuildings, reopened in the form we see it here in 1892, when on first night, Marie Lloyd topped the bill and gave a spirited rendition of *Oh Mr Porter*. The Oxford became a theatre in 1917 and was then home to a series of spectacular revues. It was demolished in 1926.

Lyons Oxford Corner House, c. 1930. Following the demise of the Oxford Theatre in 1926, the site was soon filled with a vast Lyons Corner House which was roomy enough to accommodate 2500 diners. The Lyons corner houses and tea shops could be found throughout London and enjoyed similar popularity to the modern McDonalds restaurants. As ever, fashions changed and the genteel Lyons establishments gradually closed. The entertainment business returned to the site of the Oxford Corner House, with a cinema complex in the basement from December 1977 and eventually, a Virgin Megastore, which expanded into the basement following the departure of the cinemas.

Hanway Street, *c.* 1908. A little of the atmosphere of past centuries seems to linger in Hanway Street, a narrow by-way which curves round from Oxford Street to Tottenham Court Road. A past resident was William Baker, the builder who gave his name to his own far grander creation, Baker Street (see chapter 4). Here we see the premises of A. Chadwick's Reliable Addressing Agency, who, in their role as 'circularising specialists', were no doubt responsible for some of the 'junk mail' of the day.

Tottenham Court Road from St Giles Circus, *c.* 1920. St Giles Circus was the eastern extremity of Marylebone; the buildings to the right were in Holborn, now part of the borough of Camden. Visible on the far right is the Court Playhouse, a 420 seater cinema built around 1911 on the site of Meux's Brewery. Following the Court's closure in 1928, the far grander Dominion Theatre arose on the site and opened in 1929, when films were the principal entertainment. Lavish musical stage shows take place here now. Next door, the Horseshoe Hotel still stands, but the YMCA building with its tower has been rebuilt. On the Marylebone side, left, the West End Clothiers shop occupied the Oxford Street corner, while further along past Malzy's Restaurant, was the side entrance to the Oxford Theatre, an arrangement which survives for the modern Virgin store.

Two

Edgware Road and Maida Vale

Edgware Road and Marble Arch, c. 1925. Like Oxford Street, the straightness of Edgware Road hints at its Roman origins as Watling Street, the highway from Dover to London, St Albans and onward to Holyhead. The aerial view shows Edgware Road striking north-westward (by the aircraft's wing-tip) from its crossing with Oxford Street at Marble Arch, with Bayswater Road almost hidden at the left. This was the location of the notorious Tyburn gallows, where, from the fourteenth to the eighteenth century many of London's undesirables were dispatched. The hangings were a considerable public spectacle, but from 1928 a far more refined entertainment could be had here with the arrival of the Regal (later Odeon) cinema on the Edgware Road/Oxford Street corner. The view looks into Marylebone's hinterland, with Great Cumberland Place, centre right, running northwards from Oxford Street, before the arrival of the Cumberland Hotel. The Church of the Annunciation stands out well, right, while large cleared sites at the top of the picture were awaiting the Eleventh Church of Christ Scientist (1927), Seymour Hall and Baths (1937) and Sherwood Court. Edgware Road and its continuation, Maida Vale, were the boundaries of the once separate boroughs of Paddington and Marylebone until they were united with the City of Westminster in 1965 to form a single borough.

Edgware Road from Marble Arch, *c.* 1903. The houses on the right provided a touch of Regency elegance at the Oxford Street corner before the arrival of the new Regal cinema, which opened on 29 November 1928. In deference to the site's important Roman history when an encampment guarded the crossing point of the two Roman roads, the cinema's internal decor included Roman motifs. The Regal became an Odeon during the mid-1940s and closed on 22 March 1964 to be replaced by a new Odeon which opened on 2 February 1967, together with a monster high-rise office block which does little to improve the view from Hyde Park.

Edgware Road from Marble Arch, *c.* 1926. The Odeon cinema and the adjacent shopping and office development of 1967 swallowed up the shops on the right together with Cumberland Mews which previously had accommodated the New Inn on one corner and the Church Army's publication department on the other.

Jubilee Arch, June 1897. Marylebone celebrated the Diamond Jubilee of Queen Victoria's reign on 21 June 1897 with a colourful triumphal arch which spanned Edgware Road by Upper George Street. The arch was erected at the expense of the Vestry of St Marylebone and there were decorations along Edgware Road from Marble Arch to Marylebone Road, this being part of a processional route taken by Her Majesty on Jubilee day.

Edgware Road looking towards Marble Arch, c. 1926. Although it was lined by shops, Edgware Road was a less fashionable shopping street than Oxford Street; nevertheless there were a few department stores including that of Cozens & Co. the linen drapers, whose premises were to be found by Seymour Street. Mrs Mary Pipe's Servants Registry Office was on the further Seymour Street corner.

E & R Garrould's shop, *c*. 1907. Edwin and Robert Garrould, drapers, traded from this fine row of shops which faced onto Edgware Road and ran round into Queen Street (more familiar now as Harrowby Street). One of Edgware Road's numerous small cinemas, the Connaught, would by 1913 be found at the left of the view.

Looking south from Oxford Terrace, Grand Junction Road (now Sussex Gardens), *c*. 1906. Henry Trask was landlord of the Crown pub on the Marylebone Road corner, while further along was a long-vanished side turning, Browns Court. One of its corners was occupied by W. Straker the 'very cheap stationer', while the nearer corner would soon provide the entrance to another of the neighbourhood's early cinemas, the Blue Hall Electric Theatre (see p. 64). All this property has been rebuilt at various times and many of the shops are now under Middle Eastern ownership, their Arabic shop signs giving Edgware Road its own special appeal. A large complex of flats replaced the old shops on the right during the mid-1960s.

Looking north from Marylebone Road, *c.* 1912. The terrace of shops on the right is one of the few to have resisted the developers and apart from the occupants of the shops, has changed little. Two branches of the once popular portrait photographers, USA Studios are seen here and examples of their work can still be found in quantity. A branch of Marks & Spencer, merely a single small shop, opened mid-way along the terrace in 1922. The drinking fountain, right, was on the Marylebone Road corner.

Edgware Road looking north, *c.* 1920. Travelling a little further north, the corner of Chapel Street is revealed, right, where Gardiner & Co's. Scotch House is seen with a clock tower crowning their premises. To the right, a branch of Frederick Bateman & Co., the opticians, shows their familiar 'eye' and 'spectacle' signs, while their neighbour Harry Asher, dentist, promised 'painless extractions'. Buses on still familiar routes are seen here; 6s and 16s still work the Edgware Road.

Edgware Road by Chapel Street, *c.* 1905. A branch of clothiers Charles Baker & Co. occupied the southern corner of Chapel Street, while to the right, the Kings Arms was another of the pubs run by Henry Trask and his wife.

Chapel Street from Edgware Road, *c.* 1906. Another large clothing store was to be found on the northern Chapel Street corner, Gardiner & Co. who traded under the name The Scotch House. A sailor suit was an essential part of an Edwardian boy's wardrobe and here we see a Gardiner's sales promotion for them, when, apparently, they had a quarter of a million of them in stock. The company also provided 'complete outfits for colonists and apprentices'. A large Marks & Spencer topped by a monster office block stands here now.

Edgware Road opposite Harrow Road, *c.* 1911. This is part of the long terrace of shops which once ran from Chapel Street to Bell Street (centre), most of which have been demolished to accommodate the Marylebone Flyover and its network of widened roads and subways. The flyover, part of Westway linking Marylebone Road with the Western Avenue, now rises high above the sites of the Grand Kinema (far right), G. Kemp & Sons jewellery and clock shop and a similar establishment run by George Hinds where several timepieces on ornate wrought-iron brackets gave an informative display. Next door, the building of Woolf's the tailors had almost disappeared behind a surfeit of lettering, while further along, a branch of Lilley & Skinners was adjacent to Edgware Road tube station, which still survives by the new approach to Marylebone Road. Edgware Road's most renowned place of entertainment, the Metropolitan Theatre of Varieties is in the distant left part of the photograph.

Edgware Road Tram Terminus, Harrow Road, *c.* 1935. The building of the Marylebone Flyover swept away the previously congested Harrow Road junction and all the buildings around it, one of which included the Grand Kinema with its distinctive arched facade. Marylebone is actually unique in that it was the only central London borough never to have electric trams running in any of its streets; the lines seen here terminated just short of Edgware Road on the Paddington side.

Building Marylebone Flyover, 1966. The new flyover was taking shape but had yet to make the final leap over Edgware Road and it would be another year before opening day on the 12 October 1967. Bell Street is at the left, with Edgware Road station, which appears almost unchanged since it was built.

Edgware Road by Bell Street, *c.* 1903. The same stretch of road, but a much earlier view than the previous one, shows the Green Man pub on its Bell Street corner where it survives to this day, little changed from Edwardian days when Ernest Simmonds was landlord, although the fine hanging lamps have gone. The two shops to the right of the pub, those of Sam Isaacs, fried-fish seller and Waller & Son, corn and coal merchants, would soon give up their sites for Edgware Road station on the Baker Street and Waterloo Railway's extension line from Marylebone station (then called 'Great Central'), which opened on 15 June 1907. The station, whose frontage is one of the narrowest on the London Underground, slotted neatly into its constricted site, but following the demolition of all the shops beyond it, it now has a corner position, where its restored frontage and red glazed tiling make it an attractive sight. Here, the Edgware Road pavements were typically busy and among a throng of people outside the pub, a boot-black awaits the next client. This would not be long in coming; the dusty pavements of London during dry weather and muddy conditions on wet days, ensured a ready clientele for such gentlemen.

Edgware Road by Earl Street (Broadley Street), *c.* 1906. Rather unusual vertical sunblinds are seen protecting the window displays of Counter & Co., tobacconists, on the Earl Street corner. Adjacent was the shop of Barnet Silverstone, tailor, and there was a branch of Home & Colonial Stores next door with an attractive recessed shop behind a pair of columns. Earl Street was renamed Broadley Street during the 1930s.

Edgware Road by Church Street, *c.* 1906. The clarity of this photograph reveals some tempting prices in the shop windows: a 'handsome bedstead' for £4 19s 6d in Ernest Musgrove's furniture shop; fancy hats for ladies at 4/11d and gents trousers to measure for 6/9d, courtesy of Joseph Tucker, tailor. Frank Marsh and Co. the furniture removers, occupied the large block by Church Street's southern corner, right, in a shop which would soon become a cinema. This building still stands, minus the top two floors.

Edgware Road by Church Street, c. 1910. Seen from a similar viewpoint to the previous photograph, the Edwardian tranquility has given way to a scene of chaos following the eruption of a large water main, which has torn up the wooden paving blocks and flooded the road. Locals have turned out in force to view the spectacle, forsaking the alternative pleasures of the Electric Empire cinema, whose 'finest living pictures in the world' had, by this time, replaced Frank Marsh's furniture shop by Church Street.

Edgware Road by Church Street, c. 1910. This bus, which was operated by the Great Eastern London Motor Omnibus Co. fell victim to the flood when its wheels became trapped in the damaged road surface. To the wrath of local traders, it was apparently 'an eighth of a year' before the road could be repaired and reopened for normal use. The view is of the Paddington side of the road, with the Wheatsheaf pub standing by that part of Church Street which leads to St Mary's, once the village church of Paddington.

North Street (now Frampton Street) from Edgware Road, *c.* 1904. At the beginning of the twentieth century, many of Edgware Road's side streets contained poor, overcrowded housing, a typical example being North Street, with its mixture of gloomy terraces, local shops and pubs. Here we see the south side of the street with George Garnham's Coffee House ('a good pull-up for cabmen'), adjacent to the Lord Chancellor pub on the Hatton Street corner, where its painted facade stood out against the soot-blackened brickwork of its neighbours. Some of the buildings on the right have survived, but a more modern pub, the Lord Frampton, has replaced the old one and the rest of the street has been transformed with the arrival from the 1920s of the neo-Georgian Lilestone and Fisherton housing estates.

John Morgan's grocery shop, North Street (Frampton Street) by Salisbury Street (now Fisherton Street). This was a typical local corner shop with a useful range of produce which included XL bread at $2\frac{1}{2}$d per loaf and large bottles of Whitbread's India Pale Ale at 2/6d per dozen.

Northamptonshire Bootmakers March to London, May 1905. Led by a brass band, a large group of striking army bootmakers from Northamptonshire are pictured in Edgware Road by Paddington fire station as they march to the War Office to lay before the Secretary of State for War, a request for an enquiry into the wages paid for army boots by firms who were said to have contravened a fair wages clause. The people and traders of Marylebone welcomed the marchers and a 'substantial dinner' was provided for them at the headquarters of the Marylebone branch of the Social Democratic League in Marylebone Road.

Clifton Court, Maida Vale, c. 1928. Edgware Road becomes Maida Vale at Aberdeen Place, right, and with it comes Clifton Court, a mock-Tudor extravaganza dating from the mid-1920s. This style of architecture became popular from late Victorian times, but few examples can have been as flamboyant as this.

Maida Vale by Hall Road, *c.* 1911. Vale Court, right, is typical of the handsome blocks of mansion flats which distinguish Maida Vale, but the large nineteenth-century villas on the Paddington side, left, have given way to the post-war Atholl House and other blocks of flats on the Maida Vale housing estate.

Maida Vale by St John's Wood Road, *c.* 1923. The twin-gabled building, centre, was the Hospital for Epilepsy and Paralysis, where according to the nurse who sent this postcard in 1926, the hours were long, starting at 6 am and ending at 8 pm with a two hour break during the day. The hospital was founded in 1866 in Charles Street (now Blandford Place) and moved to Maida Vale in 1903. Following closure of the hospital, the old building now stands empty.

Three
Marylebone Transport

Baker Street by Marylebone Road, c. 1905. Marylebone, because of its proximity to the cities of London and Westminster, has played an important role in the development of various forms of public transport in the capital. Several elements in the story are brought together in this historic image, as passengers crowd the top deck of a new motor-bus, then a considerable novelty at a time when nearly all London's buses were horse-drawn. This bus, a Milnes-Daimler, was owned by the London Motor Omnibus Company and briefly carried the fleetname 'Victory', before it was repainted with the name that was, for a few years, to become a familiar one on London's streets, 'Vanguard'. The horse-bus, by contrast, had attracted no passengers and its days were numbered, for it was working a route from Baker Street to Waterloo. Its successor may be seen at the extreme left of the photograph in the shape of the Baker Street and Waterloo Railway Company's new station, which was nearing completion and from 1906 electric trains would do the journey in a fraction of the time taken by the horse-bus. The new 'Bakerloo' tube would link up with Baker Street's Metropolitan station, whose original entrances dating from 1863 can be seen behind the buses. Note the narrowness of Marylebone Road, centre; there are now seven busy traffic lanes crossing Baker Street at this point.

Horse-bus, November 1869. London's first horse-buses ran from The Yorkshire Stingo in Marylebone Road to the Bank from as early as 1829. The service proved popular and soon a network of routes spread throughout the capital. This bus was the first to cross the new Holborn Viaduct on 8 November 1869 and as a momento of the event, the driver, Thomas Grayson, was presented with a silver mounted whip by Captain Cuff of Regent's Park. The bus's route was from St John's Wood, Finchley Road, Baker Street, Oxford Street and onward to the City.

Horse-buses, Edgware Road, c. 1907. A trio of buses owned by London General Omnibus Company Ltd., forerunners of London Transport.

The after-life of a horse-bus, *c.* 1912. As the Edwardian era progressed, London's fleet of horse-buses was gradually replaced by motors and while many of the old buses were scrapped, others took on new roles. This veteran of Marylebone's streets found honourable retirement in the more peaceful surroundings of a farm at Radwinter, Essex, where, minus its top deck, it provided temporary accommodation for male farmworkers. Remarkably, it still retained its old route markings from the days when it journeyed along Regent Street, Great Portland Street and, via the zoo in Regent's Park, onward to Camden Town. It was only in their last years that some horse-buses carried route numbers; this one, number 74, is still a familiar route number in Marylebone.

Scott-Stirling Motor-bus, *c.* 1904. Although the first mechanically propelled bus ran in London as early as 1833, it was not until the twentieth century that they began to appear in any quantity. Edgware Road was a favourite location for the trial running of some extraordinary contraptions, but quite successful for their early date were these single-deck Scott-Stirlings. They were operated by the London Power Omnibus Co. from 1902, with their drivers seated behind the vehicle's massive radiators. This one's advertisement, however, promotes an alternative and possibly safer method of getting to one's destination.

Upper Baker Street by Marylebone Road, *c.* 1907. By 1907, the Baker Street station area was developing into an important transport interchange, with its underground railways and numerous horse and motor bus routes. Here, a Milnes-Daimler bus operated by Tom Hearn of Dulwich takes on passengers for a journey to St John's Wood and Finchley. This one did not carry a route number, although these had been introduced on some London buses during 1906. The Globe pub can be seen beyond a former southern entrance to Baker Street station.

New Pulman Car.

The Pullman Car, Langham Place, *c.* 1908. This luxurious vehicle, one of a few operated by the General Motor Cab Company of Brixton Road, was part of a short-lived service which combined the comfort of a taxi-cab with the convenience of a bus working a fixed route. The service ran from the Langham Hotel (behind the camera), to Queen's Gate, Kensington. The flat-fare was a hefty 6d, as against the regular bus's 1d and 2d fares, but compared favourably with a motor-cab's 8d per mile.

Zeppelin Raid over London Sep^t 8th 1915. All that was left of a L.G.O. Motor Bus, after being struck by a Shell.

A number 8 bus, 8 September 1915. London's first standardised bus was the B type, of which over 3000 entered service from 1910. They were to be found on all the routes running through Marylebone, including the number 8, which still runs along Oxford Street. This example was not looking its best, having been blasted by a bomb which fell in a Zeppelin raid during the First World War.

Point Duty, Oxford Street, c. 1924. In the days before traffic lights became a familiar sight, policemen on point duty were needed to control the ever increasing motor traffic on London's roads. By this time, buses had become larger and more reliable, but the driver and top deck passengers still had little protection from bad weather.

MARYLEBONE ROAD LONDON.W.　　　　　　　　　　　　　　　FK 1249.

Baker Street Station, *c.* 1912. History was made on 10 January 1863, when the Metropolitan Railway Company opened a line between Farringdon and what was then the suburb of Paddington, with five intermediate stations including Baker Street. This was the modest beginning of the world famous London Underground, which was the first underground railway in the world. The revolutionary subterranean proved successful and from that early nucleus, a great network of new lines expanded beneath the capital and is indeed still doing so. Baker Street station now has five lines running through it, including the deep level Bakerloo tube, which opened on 10 March 1906 and the Jubilee line, which took over part of the Bakerloo service from 1 May 1979. The Hammersmith & City line and the Inner Circle use Baker Street's original platforms, where restoration during the 1980s removed decades of soot deposits, revealing the fine Victorian brickwork and old ventilation shafts, which used to clear the smoke and steam from the locomotives. The photographer has caught the station at an interesting stage of its development, soon after the removal of the old Metropolitan Railway ticket halls and with a new entrance in Portland stone, which arrived in 1911. This stood alone as we see it here for many years until the Metropolitan Railway built the massive Chiltern Court flats from 1927, which finally removed the last of the grimy terraced houses by Baker Street. The 1911 entrance was incorporated into the new building and appears now to have always been a part of it. Crowned by the noble bulk of Chiltern Court, Baker Street station presented an impressive facade to the world and was actively advertised by the Metropolitan Railway as the 'Gateway to Metroland', their word for the villages and towns along the railway line, where the company promoted extensive housing schemes.

The Bakerloo Station, Upper Baker Street, *c*. 1906. With its fine glazed terra-cotta frontage and striking design, the station was typical of London's Edwardian tube stations. When it opened on March 1906, Baker Street was briefly the terminus of the line, but on 27 March 1906 the railway was extended to Marylebone station (then called 'Great Central'), while the next section to Edgware Road did not open until 15 June 1907. The old station entrance closed in 1940, but still formed part of the street scene until demolition in 1964.

The Bakerloo Tube, *c*. 1914. It was once common practice for railway companies to issue attractive sets of postcards depicting places of interest around their stations. This example illustrates the delights of Regent's Park, easily reached from the Bakerloo line's Regent's Park Station. The line had been, by this time, extended as far as Paddington.

HIGGS & HILL
HIGGS & HILL
BAKER STREET
(Metropolitan Railway)
"GRATWORCUS"
CRANE
192 FEET HIGH.
Supplied and Erected by
SKELTON & SONS,
CATFORD, S.E.6.
Telephone: Sydenham 1584.
Revolving a complete circle
covering an area of
30,500 Sq. Ft.

Building Chiltern Court, *c.* 1927. Work begins on the new Chiltern Court above Baker Street station, a project which had been planned as early as 1913, when it was then to have been an hotel. The old terraces of Upper Baker Street are seen beyond a 192 ft high crane, with the bulk of the Edwardian Chalfont Court visible on the horizon. Chiltern Court contained 180 residential suites and notable past residents included H.G. Wells and Arnold Bennett.

St John's Road station from Wellington Road, *c.* 1905. The first stage of a new railway which would in time extend from Baker Street far into the Buckinghamshire countryside opened on 13 April 1868. This was the Metropolitan & St John's Wood Railway Co.'s line to Swiss Cottage, the first stop being St John's Wood Road. The Metropolian Railway took control of the line in 1882 and extended the line throughout the 1880s and 1890s, giving residents of parts of Middlesex, Hertfordshire and Buckinghamshire a comfortable train service to town. This is now the underground's Metropolitan line.

St John's Wood Road Station, *c.* 1906. St John's Wood Road station was renamed 'St John's Wood' on 1 April 1925 and on 11 June 1939 it took another new name, 'Lords', by reason of its proximity to that august establishment. The life of Lord's station was brief and it closed on 19 November 1939 and a new St John's Wood station opened the next day in Finchley Road. The Hilton International Hotel stands on the sites of the old station and the adjoining Red House Hotel.

Marlborough Road Station, c. 1935. The opening of the new St John's Wood station in 1939 rendered this old Metropolitan station redundant, but its surface buildings may still be seen in a new role as a restaurant. Passengers speeding along the line between Baker Street and Finchley Road may also catch a glimpse of what is left of the old platforms and arcaded walls.

Marlborough Road Station, c. 1935. A notice proclaims there was 'cricket at Lord's today', which would have added to the numbers of passengers using the station, but there was still time for the staff to pose for a photograph. Most underground stations had room for some shops and there was an Eastman's the cleaners here, with the traditional W.H. Smith & Son bookstall. The station stood at the Queens Road (now Queens Grove) corner of Finchley Road and closed on 19 November 1939.

The Hammersmith & City Railway from Edgware Road Metropolitan Station, 1906. One of the underground's last steam operated trains is seen approaching, tender first, en route for Hammersmith, just before the line was completely electrified on 3 December 1906. Edgware Road was another of the intermediate stations on the first section of the Metropolitan Railway to open in 1863, before going on to accommodate services on the Hammersmith & City Railway and the Inner Circle. It also became the terminus of a branch of the District line on 1 November 1926. A row of track-side posters is seen advertising some popular products of the day, including 'Tatcho the Great Hairgrower', Pears Soap, Liptons Tea and for those who fancied a good day out, the Austrian Exhibition at Earls Court, which was easily reached from here on the Inner Circle. The station's deep, sooty cutting was overlooked by Mitcham Street, left, where a roof-top sign pinpoints the premises of Edmund Knowles, brazier and coppersmith. The site of Mitcham Street now lays beneath the approach roads to Marylebone Flyover and Harrow Road. The distant clock tower is that of the Great Central Hotel (now the Landmark Hotel) in Marylebone Road.

Marylebone Station, *c.* 1906. Marylebone station was built by the Great Central Railway as the London terminus of their line, which was the last main line railway to be built in central London. The railway company faced hard-fought opposition to their scheme, which involved railway construction through parts of St John's Wood and other residential areas. The line and its terminus opened in 1899, having displaced old Harewood Square and many houses in Blandford Square. One side of Boston Place lost all its houses, while Dorchester Place and Boscobel Gardens were among other streets to vanish forever.

The Concourse, Marylebone Station, *c.* 1906. Marylebone was never the busiest of London's termini, but the attractive concourse appears quite animated here, with well-dressed Edwardians awaiting their trains. The season ticket office, left, has been adorned with photographs of beauty spots along the Great Central's lines, while a notice board promotes the then new Letchworth Garden City as the place to live. The tall wooden construction topped by a miniature roof, centre, informed of train departures.

The Barge Wharf, Marylebone Station, May 1917. This was the freight transfer terminal between the Great Central Railway's Marylebone station and the Regents Canal, which had opened in 1820. All signs of commercial activity have now been swept away and a pleasant canal-side walkway borders the modern flats and open spaces of the Lisson Green Estate. Cottesloe and Hughenden Houses stand close by.

OGLE MOTOR Cᴼ· Lᵀᴰ·
OGLE STREET, W.1

CAR
REPAIRS
SHOP

Tel.
MUSEUM 7869

Estimates for
REPAIRS
given Free of Charge

GARAGE. Tel. Museum 539.
44½ UPPER MARYLEBONE STREET, W.1.
DAILY DELIVERIES OF PETROL, BENZOLE & MOTOR ACCESSORIES.
Sec. G. M. COOKE-YARBOROUGH

Ogle Motor Company, Ogle Street, *c.* 1923. The popularity of private motoring increased throughout the 1920s and as car prices fell, fewer people were dependant on public transport. Garages like Ogle Motor Company catered for Marylebone's newly mobile residents with premises in Ogle Street and at 44½ Upper Marylebone Street (now New Cavendish Street). A touch of nostalgia is provided by the old 'Museum' telephone numbers.

Four

Marylebone Road and Baker Street

LONDON. Marylebone Road. No. 1882.

Marylebone Road and Baker Street, both of which were laid out during the 1750s, cross at a point sometimes known as Marylebone Circus. Marylebone Road was built as London's first northern bypass to relieve the congestion of traffic in Oxford Street. The road has played a significant part in London's transport history, with the capital's first buses running along it and the world's first underground railway rumbling beneath it. When first built, Marylebone Road was called 'The New Road' and was lined with tall terraced houses with long front gardens. The houses were replaced with a succession of notable buildings, including the Great Central Hotel, Marylebone Town Hall and Madame Tussaud's Waxworks. Baker Street is famed more for someone who never existed, Conan Doyle's fictional detective Sherlock Holmes, than for the man after whom the street was named, the speculative builder William Baker. It, too, was lined by tall terraces, some of which may still be seen. The view from around 1920 looks westward along Marylebone Road from East Street (Chiltern Street from the 1930s) and shows the gabled red-brick flats of Bickenhall Mansions (built in 1896) and one of Marylebone Road's original terraces by Upper Baker Street, where the vast Berkeley House flats would soon be built. Baker Street station is on the right.

Marylebone Road by Edgware Road, *c.* 1956. The showrooms of antique dealer P.C.L. German were laid out over the front gardens of one of Marylebone Road's old terraces, but its site and those of the adjoining Blue Hall Cinema and the Crown pub (see page 38) would soon be taken by a grim office block. Following the opening of the Marylebone Flyover, this road was renamed Old Marylebone Road.

The Church of Our Lady of the Rosary, *c.* 1908. Built in 1870, this Roman Catholic church was situated beside the narrow Homer Row until it was replaced by a new church in 1963 on the site of the house on the right. The Rosary Hall was constructed on the site of the old church.

Marylebone Road by Harcourt Street from Chapel Street, *c.* 1905. Two vanished landmarks are pictured on either side of Harcourt Street: Paddington Chapel, a congregational chapel built in 1813 and refronted in 1899 and Queen Charlotte's Hospital, left. The hospital was founded in 1752 and moved to the Old Manor House, Lisson Green, in 1813. In 1856 and 1886 it was rebuilt to look as it does in this picture. The hospital moved to Hammersmith in 1929. Office blocks now cover the sites of both establishments and that of William Woodrow, carriage builder, right.

Marylebone Grammar School, *c.* 1903. Founded as the Philological School during 1792 in Fitzroy Square, the school moved to this site beside Lisson Grove in 1827. Notable 'old boys' include novelists Len Deighton and Jerome K. Jerome of *Three Men in a Boat* fame. Following the school's closure in 1981, the best of the distinctive gothic buildings were preserved as part of a new office complex dating from 1989.

Hotel Great Central, *c*. 1904. The building of the Great Central Railway into Marylebone included this fine railway hotel, its red brick and terra-cotta finish matching in a more grandiose way that of the station at the rear, to which it was linked by an elegant *porte cochère*. Following the closure of the hotel, the building found a new role as a transit camp during the Second World War and was also used as the headquarters for various departments of the British Transport Commission. Restoration to hotel use from 1989/91 revealed again the splendour of the building with its tall clock tower. The hotel is now known as The Landmark.

Hotel Great Central, *c*. 1904. The impressive bulk of the hotel rises behind a Hansom cab waiting on its rank. The houses on the right were typical of Marylebone Road, but these had already lost their residential status and were in use by departments of the Great Central Railway. The national Cash Register offices (built in 1936) are here now.

Great Central Filling Station, Marylebone Road, *c.* 1928. The short terrace between Knox Street, left, and Wyndham Street, right, had also lost its residents, with various businesses making good use of the generous front gardens of the old houses. Kelly & Co., the monumental masons had plenty of room for a display of their products, while the frontages of three houses comfortably accommodated the Great Central Filling station, a name borrowed from the railway company on the opposite side of the road. The filling station was evidently a popular call for taxis, with three of them visible here, filling up with some brands of fuel which included 'National Benzole Mixture' and 'Power Petrol'. In time, the ever increasing motor traffic would necessitate road widening schemes in Marylebone Road, with the old narrow carriageways expanding to an ever more congested six lanes, as the popularity of the road as an east/west route threatened to overwhelm the area in traffic. Offices for British Home Stores were built here in 1939. (Tony Davies, Marylebone Gallery)

Bickenhall Mansions, *c.* 1905. The building of these impressive mansion flats in 1896 removed another of Marylebone Road's old terraces and small streets at the rear, including Great York Mews and Little York Place. The road had already been widened in front of the flats, but to the right of Gloucester Place, centre, the long front gardens still extended into what are now busy traffic lanes. Marylebone's new Town Hall was built here from 1914.

Marylebone Town Hall and Bickenhall Mansions, *c.* 1922. The foundation stone of the new Town Hall was laid on 7 July 1914 by the Princess Royal, Duchess of Fife, but having been commandeered for Government purposes during the First World War, the building was not formally opened until 27 March 1920, when Prince Albert (later King George VI) performed the ceremony. The building was designed by Sir Edwin Cooper and is now known as Westminster Council House following Marylebone's amalgamation with Westminster and Paddington in 1965.

Marylebone Road from East Street (Chiltern Street), *c.* 1903. Here is a lively slice of Edwardian street life, with a jostle of Hansoms, carriages, vans and a bootblack with a client on the pavement by East Street. A cockney flower girl with her basket balanced on her head, leaves the refuge of the traffic island and makes a hazardous crossing of the eastbound carriageway (busy even at this early date), towards Baker Street station. Part of Portman Mansions are seen on the right by East Street (Chiltern Street), but further along, the gabled flats were replaced by buildings for the Polytechnic of Central London, now Westminster University.

Madame Tussaud's Waxworks, c. 1904. One of Marylebone's most famous institutions and one of London's most popular tourist attractions began in a modest way when Madame Marie Tussaud left France for England in 1802 bringing with her a collection of wax figures which she used as the basis of a travelling show. She established a permanent exhibition in Baker Street in 1835, but died in 1850 aged 90. The still expanding exhibition continued under the guidance of her descendants and in 1884 it moved to these fine new premises in Marylebone Road. Madame Tussaud's former neighbours in 1904 included the Buffalo's Head pub by Allsop Place, while next door was still in residential use and there was a flat to be let within. These buildings vanished with the rebuilding of Baker Street station's frontage.

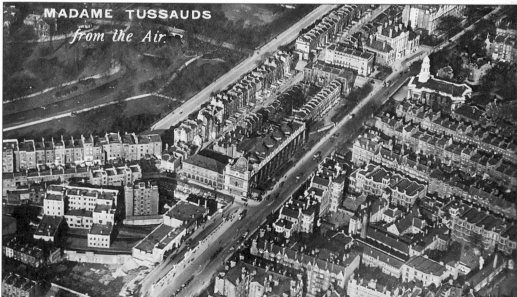

Madame Tussaud's and Marylebone Road from the air, c. 1920. Many local landmarks can be picked out here, including Baker Street station as it was prior to the Chiltern Court development. Also visible is Marylebone parish church with its white tower, right, and the former workhouse by the site of the present university buildings. Regent's Park is at the top of the picture.

LONDON. Madame Tussauds. No. 1023.

Madame Tussaud's, *c.* 1920. The view from near Nottingham Place reveals the tall, creeper clad walls of Madame Tussaud's before the building was destroyed by fire in 1925. The then narrow Marylebone Road still had leafy gardens on its southern side, left.

Madame Tussauds. N.W.   121500.

Madame Tussaud's Cinema, *c.* 1929. There was also a 300 seater cinema at Madame Tussaud's from as early as 1909, when visitors could view 'free displays of topical moving pictures'. The catastrophic fire of March 1925 led to the development of the new building we see here, with its 1714 seater cinema, which opened on 26 April 1928. The 'forthcoming attraction' notices highlight some of the stars of the day, with Bebe Daniels in *She's a Sheik* and Lon Chaney in *The Unknown*. There were also live acts on stage. The cinema was destroyed by bombing during September 1940, but from 1957 there was a new attraction here, the London Planetarium.

St Mary, Marylebone, *c.* 1910. The ancient parish church of the hamlet of Marylebone stood near Tyburn Road (Oxford Street) before a new church was built in the High Street around 1400. As the eighteenth century progressed, it became obvious that a larger parish church would be needed for the rapidly increasing population, but it was not until February 1817 that a new church, built to the designs of Thomas Hardwick, was ready for its worshippers. The Edwardian view shows the church to have been comfortably distant from the traffic that now thunders by close to its Corinthian colonnade.

St Mary, Marylebone, *c.* 1920. The view from High Street (now Marylebone High Street), reveals more of the distinctive architectural style of St Mary's church. The marriage of poets Robert Browning and Elizabeth Barrett took place here in 1846.

The Royal Academy of Music, c. 1920. Marylebone Road is notable for its fine buildings, a handsome example of which is the Royal Academy of Music, which was formally opened in June 1912 by Prince Arthur of Connaught. The Academy was founded in 1822 by Lord Burghersh, eleventh Earl of Westmoreland and then occupied a single house in Tenterden Street, Hanover Square. Other houses were added, but when the Academy outgrew them, it moved to Marylebone Road, where the St Marylebone Charity School for Girls had previously stood.

Harley House, c. 1920. The noble city-scape of Marylebone Road is typified by these Edwardian mansion flats, which have retained their leafy frontage despite the demands of ceaseless modern traffic.

73

St Marylebone Church of England School, *c. 1906*. The school's buildings date from 1863 and 1894 and stand adjacent to St Mary's church, right. This jolly group of youngsters in smocks and black stockings played through an Edwardian afternoon happily unaware of the controversy to come during the 1930s, with plans to create a new playground for their successors on the old burial ground of St Marylebone Chapel, the former parish church (behind the camera). The scheme involved the moving of memorial stones, including that of Charles Wesley, hymnwriter and brother of John Wesley, the founder of Methodism.

Marylebone Road by Park Crescent, *c. 1906*. An early motor car heads towards the Park Square East Gate of Regent's Park, where the intricate ironwork and crown-topped gas lamps then made an impressive entrance to the park. Part of Park Crescent is on the right with, centre, the tower of Holy Trinity Church which was built from 1826/8, long before it became overshadowed by the sky-scraping commercial tower blocks of Euston.

Upper Baker Street, c. 1906. This was the former name of the short section of Baker Street to the north of Marylebone Road, but Allsop Street, centre, vanished completely when the flats and shops of Berkeley Court were built here in 1928. These late eighteenth-century properties then accommodated Frederick Cooper, stationer, whose windows were filled with an alluring display of Edwardian postcards, while to the right was Benjamin Vandersluis's fish shop and his delivery cart parked in Allsop Street. Sidney Klosz, grocer, traded from the single storey shop on the Marylebone Road corner, left.

Upper Baker Street, c. 1906. The side road was New Street, more familiar now as Melcombe Street. The construction of Berkeley Court also removed the corner shop, left, then a branch of Bravington's, the pawnbrokers and jewellers. The houses and shops beyond New Street were replaced by the magnificent Abbey National Building Society headquarters, which were opened on 18 March 1932 by Prime Minister Ramsay MacDonald. Upper Baker Street post office had previously stood in New Street, with Frederick Pitt's grocery shop taking the corner position. Webster & Girling, the ticket agents, were next door.

New Street (Melcombe Street) from Dorset Square, c. 1904. Shops in New Street, with New Street Mews (Chagford Street), centre. Further along, some very dilapidated property was awaiting demolition, and replacement with blocks of smart mansion flats, Clarence Gate Gardens. Contractor's hoardings had already been erected around the old Hope Tavern on the Glentworth Street corner. Upper Baker Street is in the distance.

New Street (Melcombe Street) from Upper Baker Street, c. 1910. Clarence Gate Gardens had arrived, right, with a more flamboyant style to contrast with the plain eighteenth-century terraces. The houses on the left with another tiny side turning, Little Park Street, still had a few more years life in them before eventual replacement with the stylish Berkeley Court and Dorset House apartment blocks.

Upper Baker Street, c. 1906. These were more of Upper Baker Street's original houses, which by Edwardian times had been taken over by a variety of commerical enterprises, including Miss Hooper's Institute for Trained Nurses, George Head and Co. auctioneers and Bernard Klein, hairdresser, chiropodist and manicurist, where one could have a shave for 2d and a haircut for 4d. Chiltern Court stands here now.

York Place (Baker Street), by Marylebone Road, c. 1903. The section of road between Marylebone Road and Dorset Street was previously known as York Place before the whole street was unified with the single name, Baker Street. The viewpoint is similar to that of the photograph on page 49, but in this slightly earlier picture, the horse-bus is king, and the gathering of buses would have made a colourful sight with their different coloured liveries and advertisements. The red and white Hudson's soap advertisement on the second bus was a familiar one on many of London's horse-buses.

York Place (Baker Street), by Portman Mansions (Porter Street), *c*. 1903. A Hansom cab, a gas lamp, a long row of grey terraced houses disappearing into a sepia-coloured murk: this was the Baker Street of Sherlock Holmes in a contemporary photograph which captures something of the atmosphere of the foggy city so vividly described in the words of Sir Arthur Conan Doyle.

York Place (Baker Street), *c*. 1904. This section of Baker Street was residential, with tall town houses distinguished by their round-headed first floor windows. Many of them, or later replicas, may still be seen above the shops which now occupy their ground floors. The Sherlock Holmes Hotel is also here, perpetuating the imagery of the street's famous fictional inhabitant. Statesman William Pitt the younger lived in one of these houses early in the nineteenth century, having attained the post of Prime Minister in 1783 when he was a youthful twenty-four, a post he retained for seventeen years.

Baker Street, *c.* 1903. The long terrace between King Street (Blandford Street) and Dorset Street included the Portman Rooms, which housed Madame Tussaud's waxworks during their sojourn in Baker Street. The Portman Rooms were also used for social gatherings, but their destruction during an air raid on 10 May 1941 preceded the development of the site as the headquarters of Marks & Spencer. A well-known Baker Street business, Messrs Druce & Co., was based here.

Baker Street looking south, *c.* 1920. Postwar rebuilding has transformed this scene, from which nothing remains. Marks & Spencer's headquarters have taken the place of the terrace on the right, while the long row of shops running down to Blandford Street is now uncompromisingly modern in appearance.

Baker Street by Dorset Street, c. 1904. To the right was the shop of Francis Green, tailor and supplier of naval and military uniforms, while on the further corner, it was sale time at H.E. Randall's boot and shoe shop. The tall house behind the carriage in Dorset Street were the premises of Charles Franklin, coal merchant. The old terraces have long given way to modern counterparts.

Dobrin Restaurant, Baker Street, c. 1935. A clever photo-montage of this 'high class continental cafe', which stood at the Baker Street/Portman Mews North (Portman Close) corner. The neon name sign represented the height of modernity in the 1930s, but there are merely modern offices on the site now.

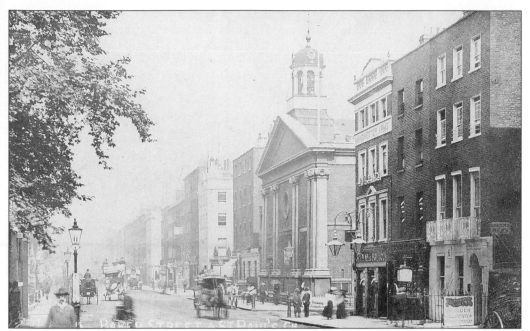

St Paul's Church, Portman Square, Baker Street, c. 1906. This was the east side of Baker Street looking north from Bakers Mews, right. St Paul's church was built in 1779 and demolished early in the 1970s. The Manchester Arms pub was on the Adam (later Robert Adam) Street corner, while the trees on the left were part of the garden of one of the grand houses of Portman Square.

St Paul's Church, Portman Square, c. 1957. St Paul's church was still standing, but demolition nearby had opened up a view of Robert Adam Street. The new St Paul's church was built in Robert Adam Street in 1970 to replace the old one. A couple on the pavement by Bakers Mews seem unperturbed by the nightmarish cinema poster beside them.

Portman Square from Baker Street and Lower Berkeley Street (Fitzhardinge Street), *c.* 1906. Portman Square, once one of Marylebone's most aristocratic garden squares, is at the southern end of Baker Street. The square was named after William Henry Portman of Orchard Portman, Somerset, who developed the square on his Marylebone estate from 1764. The Portman family had been landowners in Marylebone since the mid-1500s. Twentieth-century buildings have mostly replaced the old town houses and on this, the northern side of the square, modern flats and offices predominate.

Portman Square, *c.* 1904. The eastern side of Portman Square is shown here, where its original eighteenth-century houses stood until 1927, when demolition was followed by the construction of Orchard Court, an eight-storey block of flats. Portman Court was built on the south side of the square in a similar style. Part of Wigmore Street is on the right.

Five

A Marylebone Miscellany

Earl Street (Broadley Street) from Lisson Grove, c. 1906. Marylebone is remarkable for the sheer number of its streets to have been renamed during the present century. Three of them are on view here: Earl Street, which became Broadley Street; the narrow Little Grove Street, centre right, became Plympton Street; and Exeter Street, centre, was renamed Ashbridge Street, all during the 1930s. Another tiny side turning, Dukes Mews at the far left, has vanished altogether. The view reveals Earl Street to have been a considerable shopping street in earlier days, but various schemes of urban renewal have changed the road into one of municipal flats and gardens. Modern low-rise housing has replaced the shops on the left and, further along, the flats of the Wilcove Estate were opened in 1934 by the then Duchess of York (Queen Elizabeth, the Queen Mother). Much of the terrace on the right is still standing, but the shops have gone and the ground floors are mostly residential now. The Exeter Arms still stands on the Ashbridge Street corner, providing a link with that street's former name.

Nightingale Street from Capland Street (Gateforth Street), 1902. With an attractive name not matched by its architecture, Nightingale Street, a narrow by-way behind the shops of Church Street, was one of the borough's more notorious slums. It appeared on one of the Booth Poverty maps of 1889, in which the streets were colour-coded to indicate their status. Nightingale Street was awarded the black colour denoting 'the lowest grade' and that 'semi-criminal' classes lived here. The photographer has captured Nightingale Street in its last year, with most of the houses and shops boarded up in readiness for the demolition which would soon follow. The handful of shops were of the most basic kind: that on the left in Capland Street was James Bradley's horse meat shop, while the boarded up premises in Nightingale Street had once sold coal. A further shop (out of view) had scraped a living by selling firewood. One of the boarded up windows shows some of the graffiti of yesteryear; the scribblings were then applied in chalk, which was much easier to remove than the spray can horrors of today. The children in the photograph look well clothed and have probably come from less poverty stricken streets nearby to pose for the photographer. The wagon outside the coal shop, however, was in a bad way, having lost a wheel. This part of Capland Street is now Gateforth Street and the scene today shows Westminster Council's Gateforth Street centre and the Cockpit Theatre, which was built here during the 1970s. (London Metropolitan Archives)

Nightingale Street Buildings from Salisbury Street, *c.* 1910. The slums of Nightingale Street were swept away to be replaced in 1904 by Nightingale Street Buildings, model dwellings built through the philanthropy of Lord Portman. The buildings are still here and are now known as Morris House.

Church Street from Lisson Grove, *c.* 1906. Church Street is noted for its lively market and trendy antiques and collector's emporia, while its western end towards Edgware Road is dominated by its great municipal housing estates. To the right, the Duke of York pub (rebuilt in 1932) stands at the Capland Street (Gateforth Street) corner, while the windows of the houses on the further corner peep out through a mess of advertisements beside Benjamin Dimond's cheese shop. To the left is the tiny covered entrance to Little Grove Street (Plympton Street), with the showroom of John Nodes, undertakers, further along, and a long vanished pub, The Mitre, on the Exeter Street (Ashridge Street) corner. In later years, these shops were occupied by William Jordan, clothiers, but are now home to a remarkable establishment called Alfie's Market, a fascinating rambling complex of antiques and collector's galleries.

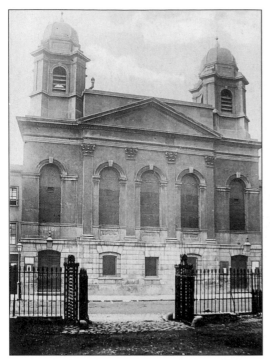

St Matthew's Church, Carlisle Street (Penfold Street), *c.* 1895. With an aspect more theatrical than ecclesiastical, this grandiose 1600 seater church stood, before war damage led to its demolition, in the midst of what is now the Church Street Estate. Colne and Kennet Houses now stand close by. The foreground gates led into Portman Market, a nineteenth-century complex for fish, meat and vegetables, with its own abbatoirs. Wytham House stands here now.

Spencer, Turner & Boldero, Drapers, Lisson Grove, 1906. Residents of Earl House, Lisson Grove may be surprised to see that a popular department store once flourished on the site of their flats. The store was founded in 1840 in what was then a popular shopping area and expanded into long frontages to Lisson Grove on both sides of Duke Street, left, where the company warehouses were situated. Duke Street was renamed Boldero Street after the store's John Boldero, but following the shop's closure in the 1960s, that street disappeared when the new flats were built over it.

Joseph Richter's Bakery, Homer Row, c. 1905. This old-fashioned bakery stood on the Homer Row/Crawford Street corner, until the whole block of buildings was replaced by Crawford Mansions in 1915.

Fitter Brothers, Butchers, Seymour Place/York Street, c. 1908. Mr and Mrs Fitter stand proudly in their doorway, surrounded by their stock, staff, and assorted delivery vehicles. Meat and poultry were often displayed in this spectacular way early in the century, before the days of electric refrigeration. The small turning at the left was Little Harcourt Street, renamed Shillibeer Place in the 1930s after George Shillibeer, who initiated London's first bus service in 1829. The buses and their horses were stabled nearby, and ran from the Yorkshire Stingo pub in Marylebone Road to the Bank of England in the City.

Upper George Street (George Street), c. 1906. This was the former name of the western part of George Street, from Montagu Square to Edgware Road. The north side of the road with the then newly rebuilt St Marylebone Presbyterian Church (1905) and typical early Marylebone town houses, led on to the later Cumberland Mansions by Brown Street. The church and houses nearest the camera now have the Marriott, a towering modern hotel, on their sites, while the houses as far as Brown Street were replaced in 1936 by the Fursecroft apartment block.

Upper Berkeley Street by Montagu Square, c. 1905. These pages contain photographs of numerous terraces with their houses intact in Edwardian times, but which, by reason of war damage or redevelopment, have had their uniformity destroyed by the insertion of later structures, often with scant regard for the scale of their neighbours. The reverse happened here when the demolition of the stone fronted Brunswick Chapel (built in 1795) with its grand pediment, led to replacement by a trio of houses, which proved a good match for the rest of the row, creating a fine long terrace which still exists.

Gloucester Street (Gloucester Place), c. 1905. The southern part of Gloucester Place was once known as Gloucester Street and was laid out around 1790 with long rows of terraced houses stretching to the point of monotony beyond Marylebone Road. Despite appearances, the block now on the far side of George Street, centre, is not the one we see in this view. The old houses were demolished and a facsimile facade with blackened brickwork to perfectly match the surrounding houses, was erected in 1977. Portman Mews North (Portman Close) is on the right.

Montagu Square from (Upper) George Street, c. 1905. Montagu Square and neighbouring Bryanston Square were developed by the Portman estate early in the nineteenth century and show variations of the usual flat-fronted Marylebone houses, with bow and bay windows to get the best of the outlook over the central gardens in the extremely elongated squares. Author Anthony Trollope found Montagu Square an agreeable place to live during the 1870s.

Great Cumberland Place by Seymour Street, *c.* 1905. These were further houses from late in the eighteenth century, built as the Portman estate's developments spread relentlessly across the fields to the north of Tyburn Road (Oxford Street). Most of the houses had plain brick fronts, but these rather grander ones were ornamented with Ionic pilasters, and some fancy ironwork around the balconies. Bilton Towers, the modern flats built on the sites of the nearer houses, are a poor match for the surviving houses at the further end of the row.

Great Cumberland Place, *c.* 1905. There was to have been another crescent facing this one to make a complete circus, but sadly, it was never built. Although these houses have been rebuilt, the style is in sympathy with the originals with a most attractive result. The modern buildings include the Montcalm Hotel and the Western Marble Arch Synagogue.

Duke Street from Oxford Street, *c.* 1905. This postcard is actually an advertisement sent by a local wholesaler, Seeley's Library of Paddington Street (see page 98) to Wood Bros., the grocery shop in the centre of the view, offering to supply further copies of this picture for 15s per hundred, for advertising purposes. Among Wood Bros. neighbours was Walter Fair's hairdressing salon, right, where a lady could have had a haircut for 6d. Part of Barrett Street, with the Red Lion pub on the corner, is to the left behind the cart. Everything here has since been rebuilt.

Wigmore street from Mandeville Place, *c.* 1904. Wigmore Street runs parallel with Oxford Street and was named after Wigmore Castle, Herefordshire, the seat of the Earls of Oxford, the local landowners who built up this area during the eighteenth century. Edwardian Wigmore Street contained numerous dressmakers amd milliners and several piano makers had their showrooms here. The view is of the north side of the street, with the narrow entrance to Jason Court marked by the shop of Ernest Gems, basketmaker, in a plain eighteenth-century building which was on the point of replacement with the picturesque structure we know today.

Marylebone Lane from Wigmore Street, c. 1907. Narrow, winding Marylebone Lane pre-dates the grids of the eighteenth-century streets which surround it, hinting at its more distant origins as a true village street, its course dictated by that of the Tyburn stream beside whose waters Marylebone came into being. Marylebone's first church stood near here until 1400 and the Town Hall was in the distant part of the view until it was replaced by the twentieth-century splendour of its successor in Marylebone Road. The view looks south towards Oxford Street and shows the former Police Station, centre.

Thayer Street from George Street, c. 1906. Another late Georgian street, with the tower of the Methodist church, Hinde Street (1881/7) peeping over the earlier terraces. Most of the old houses now have modern replacements built to a similar scale, thus preserving the flavour of the street. In yet another name change, William Street, left, became Bulstrode Street.

Post Office, 29 Thayer Street, *c.* 1909. 'How do you like the little village post office?' writes the sender of this postcard in a message which also refers to a new craze, aviation, and to pictures of Mr Wright's airship on display in Oxford Street. Thayer Street post office is now situated next door as part of a branch of Ryman's, the stationers.

Ford's Hotel, Manchester Street, *c.* 1907. Ford's Hotel stood out from its neighbours, having been built in red brick rather than the usual yellow London brick of this area. The building is now known as Hannah House and was once a staff canteen for Marks & Spencer, who still own it. The houses on the right have been replaced with flats.

Adam Street (Robert Adam Street), *c.* 1907. With the closure of St Paul's church, Portman Square (Baker Street), a replacement church arose on the site of the houses on the right. It is now called St Paul's, Robert Adam Street, and it opened in 1970. The street name commemorates Robert Adam, architect, whose local work included houses in Portman Square.

George Street, *c.* 1920. The glory of George Street is the Roman Catholic Church of St James, Spanish Place, whose cathedral-like internal magnificence is only hinted at by its rather obscured exterior. The church was designed by Edward Goldie, partly completed in 1890 and finished by 1918. The church was built to replace the chapel of the Spanish Embassy, which had previously stood at the corner of Spanish Place and Charles Street, the old name for the eastern part of George Street. To the left is the well-known Durrants Hotel, pictured here as the original hotel was expanding into further houses in the terrace.

Hertford House, Manchester Square, *c.* 1906. Manchester Square was laid out in 1776, with Hertford House, which was built for the Duke of Manchester, taking up much of the square's northern side. Hertford House is famed now as the home of the Wallace Collection, the art collection of Sir Richard Wallace, son of the fourth Marquess of Hertford. The house was extended from 1872/82 to accommodate the collection, which has been on public view since that time.

Manchester Square by Duke Street, c. 1905. Manchester Square has retained many of its Georgian houses and this scene, apart from its absence of traffic, has changed little. Some characters from yesteryear are seen here, with a flower-man standing by Duke Street as he struggles to balance his well-filled basket on his head. The sand-bin on the left has attracted a trio of youths, one of whom has managed to climb inside it.

Manchester Street from Blandford Street, c. 1905. At first sight, these houses appear little changed today, although there is no longer a corner shop; but it is all an illusion, for behind the preserved and restored facades is the modern development of Admiral Court. A Civic Trust award was bestowed in 1993 for this fine example of conservation. Admiral Sir Francis Beaufort, whose scale of wind speeds is familiar to meteorologists and mariners alike, lived at number 51 from 1822/32.

Blandford Street looking east, *c.* 1907. A few of the eighteenth-century houses on the right are still with us, but the block on the Manchester Street corner, then with George Cornwell & Sons Electric Machine Bakery, has gone. The terrace on the left has also gone, but the Lincoln Hotel, far left, has been rebuilt with an eye-catching half-timbered frontage.

Blandford Street looking West, *c.* 1907. The left-hand terrace has also been preserved as part of the Admiral Court development maintaining the eighteenth-century style of the street. The Wallace Head pub on the East Street (Chiltern Street) corner, however, has a modern replacement. Blandford Street was named after Blandford Forum, Dorset, where the Portman family who developed these estates had their family seat. Michael Faraday, founder of the science of electro-magnetism, was born nearby in Jacobs Well Mews and was apprenticed to a stationer and bookbinder at the shop to the right of this view.

Paddington Street from Baker Street, c. 1904. To the left was Seeley's Library, owned by Miss Mary Seeley, with its large stocks of picture postcards, the collection of which was then the latest craze. The old Apollo Tavern by East Street (Chiltern Street) is seen in the middle of the view, with a long terrace leading towards the former St George's burial grounds. They were opened on 6 July 1886 as Paddington Street Gardens by Princess Louise, daughter of Queen Victoria. There is now a cafe-bar, shops and a multi-storey car park on the site of the Apollo and its neighbours and York Mews South (left) was renamed Sherlock Mews in honour of the local, if fictional, detective.

Paddington Street from Northumberland Street (Luxborough Street), c. 1906. Paul Friebe was landlord at the Pitt's Head pub, left, which stood on the Northumberland Street corner. The small shops further along were replaced in 1910 by the Central Institute for Swedish Gymnastics building which still stands and is now the Hellenic Centre. The trees of Paddington Street Gardens are on the right, while the distant terrace beyond conceals one of London's tiniest byways, Grotto Passage.

East Street (Chiltern Street) from Blandford Street, c. 1906. The gothic style fire station, centre, was built in 1889 and still graces Chiltern Street, but the stucco-fronted Wallace Head pub has been rebuilt. The tall red brick and terra-cotta blocks of Wendover House date from 1891.

High Street, c. 1906. During the 1930s, the London County Council embarked upon a programme of street renaming to avoid the confusion caused by duplicated street names. 'High Street' was one of the most repeated names in the capital, but the problem was easily solved by prefixing it with the name of each locality. Thus was 'Marylebone High Street' born. The view from the beginning of the present century looks remarkably similar to the scene today, with the Lord Tyrawley pub (now the Prince Regent) with its turret still adorning the Nottingham Street corner. The High Street is one of the oldest thoroughfares in Marylebone and in the far distant part of the photograph there is just a glimpse of the old parish church, which dated from 1400. There is a memorial garden there now.

High Street by Weymouth Street, *c*. 1906. The Edwardian fashion of filling a shop window with as many products as possible is well demonstrated here, with this display by J. Smith & Son, tailors. Little daylight could have penetrated this mass of garments, which included 'very special felt hats' at 3/6d and shirt fronts at 6d each. There was a useful range of household products available next door at the Marylebone Bazaar. Marylebone post office was later built on this site, but has since moved away.

The International Tea Company, 21 High Street, *c*. 1917. There were towering displays of canned fruit in the bow-windowed shopfront of this popular chain store, as the staff pose for their picture from which cheeky boys on the left are not to be left out. The street lamp has been masked during the partial blackout of the First World War, when air raids from German Zeppelins were a constant threat.

New Cavendish Street from High Street, *c.* 1920. First laid out during the 1770s, this part of New Cavendish Street was mostly rebuilt in the late 1800s and early 1900s, the more ornate styles of that era contrasting with the plain Georgian architecture of surrounding streets. It was a high-class shopping area and there would have been good business for the cabs on their rank. A large branch of Lilley & Skinners occupied the corner premises by High Street, left.

High Street from Little Barlow Street (Vincent Street), *c.* 1920. Although the premises on the right have been rebuilt, the replacements have been on a similar scale, so the appearance of the street with its small but high class shops has been well preserved and almost a village atmosphere prevails to this day.

High Street by South Street (Blandford Street), *c.* 1880. William Gayler's corner shop was an early manifestation of a popular local department store which, under the name of Gayler & Pope, lasted until 1958. Further shops in the row included those of Webb & Co., scalemakers, William Plock, ham and beef dealer and John Winsland, oilman. Those shops would soon be rebuilt, but the corner building still stands and, as a testimony to the quality of Victorian paint, the long defunct street name for South Street can still be discerned.

High Street from Blandford Street, *c.* 1906. A profusion of lamps highlight Gayler & Pope's store, left, while the neighbouring shops in the photograph above had by this time been rebuilt.

Harley Street, *c.* 1905. Harley Street was built up from the 1750s and was for many years a street of highly fashionable town houses. Sir Arthur Wellesley (the Duke of Wellington) lived here, as did Gladstone, Turner, the landscape artist and Lady Nelson, widow of Viscount Horatio Nelson. Harley Street's world-wide fame as a centre of the medical profession dates from around the 1840s when doctors began to colonise the street, whose spacious houses and central location were ideal for their private consulting rooms.

Wimpole Street from Henrietta (Henrietta Place), *c.* 1906. Another centre of the medical profession, Wimpole Street, was named after Wimpole, the Cambridgeshire seat of Edward Harley, Earl of Oxford. The houses were built from the 1750s and Elizabeth Barratt lived at number 50 before her famous elopement with Robert Browning in 1846. The houses on the left have all gone and Mill Hill Place, centre, has been built over.

St Peter, Vere Street, *c.* 1906. This is the oldest surviving church in Marylebone, dating from 1721/4 when it was known as Oxford Chapel. It was designed by James Gibbs and was built to serve the residents of the streets then being built to the north of Oxford Street. James Gibbs' more famous creation was his rebuilt St Martin-in-the-Fields, the interior of which has been likened to a larger version of St Peter, Vere Street.

The Western District Post Office, Vere Street, *c.* 1906. A gathering of postmen, telegraph boys and parcel postmen with their handcart outside the head post office for this part of London. The post office would soon move away to Wimpole Street and a Barclays Bank would take over the old premises. St Peter's Church is out of sight behind the shops.

Cavendish Square from Harley Street, *c.* 1906. Development to the north of Oxford Street began with the laying out of Cavendish Square in 1717, but the actual houses came rather later. The corner house by Harley Street, left, was built from 1724/31, but the handsome pair of stone-fronted Palladian mansions on either side of Deans Yard (Deans Mews), did not arrive until 1769/72.

Cavendish Square, *c.* 1906. A 'growler' (four wheel cab), and a Hansom await their next fares on Cavendish Square's south side. The square's central garden is now a public open space and a welcome green oasis in this heavily built up part of town. The greenery was slightly eroded when an underground car park was built in 1971.

Upper Regent Street and All Souls Church, c. 1904. Edwardian Upper Regent Street had still retained its original Nash terraces, but these would soon be replaced by the grander structures we know today. All the vehicles were horse-drawn here and the long line of cabs ensured there was plenty of transport for those who could afford it.

All Souls Church, Langham Place, c. 1905. All Souls Church was designed in 1820 by John Nash as part of his grand Regent Street scheme to link Carlton House, the palace of the Prince Regent, with the then new Regent's Park. The elegant spire and rounded portico gave the northward view up Regent Street a focal point and beautifully handled the street's awkward dog-leg through Langham Place into Portland Place. Regrettably, that view has been ruined by the modern slab blocks that now fill the sky behind the spire. The large house on the left was built from 1780/3 by noted architect James Wyatt, but in 1931/2 its site was taken by a building which became famous worldwide: the BBC's Broadcasting House.

Queen's Hall and St George's Hall, Langham Place. These neighbouring concert halls once stood adjacent to All Souls Church, left. Queen's Hall was distinguished by its curving classical frontage, with its caryatids and busts of composers. The Henry Wood Promenade Concerts had their origin here, following Henry Wood's appointment in 1895 as conductor of the Queen's Hall orchestra. The hall was destroyed by bombing in 1941 and the 'proms' moved to their present home, the Albert Hall. St George's Hall opened in 1867 and from 1905 became famous as 'Maskelyne's Home of Mystery', where the magic show initiated by illusionist John Nevil Maskelyne could be seen. From 1934, the hall was used by the BBC for studio concerts until 1941, when it too succumbed to the bomb which destroyed its neighbour. St George's Hotel is here now.

Great Portland Street, c. 1920. This long street running from Oxford Street to Marylebone Road, changes character along its length, being a centre of the fashion industry at its southern end and something of a medical centre in the north, where several specialist hospitals have been established. The popular Pagani's Restaurant, centre, was to be found between Little Portland Street and Mortimer Street, until a German bomb flattened it in September 1940.

Portland Chapel, Great Portland Street, *c.* 1906. Pictured in the last year of its life, this chapel was built in 1776 and like St Peter, Vere Street which is similar in appearance, was provided for the new residents of the fast developing areas north of Oxford Street. The Hansom cabby has found a moment to read his newspaper.

The Philharmonic Hall, Great Portland Street, *c.* 1920. Originally known as the St James' Hall, this was another concert hall in this rather musical area and was built in 1907 on the island site of the old Portland chapel. Concerts, lectures and films were on offer here and in 1920, Sir Ernest Shackleton, the polar explorer, gave a lecture here illustrated by his own (silent) film. The hall still stands, having been converted to offices in 1930. The modernised Portland Hotel can be seen further along.

The Portland Hotel, Great Portland Street, by Gildea Street, *c.* 1904. This large hotel stood facing the Portland Chapel and its successor, the Philharmonic Hall, but it would soon acquire the modernised frontage seen in the preceding photograph. There were some very drab houses beyond the hotel and these would soon by replaced by smart new buildings more in keeping with a main road in London's West End. The hotel closed in 1935.

The Royal National Orthopaedic Hospital, *c.* 1940. The hospital stood at the northern end of Great Portland Street and occupied a large stone-fronted building dating from 1909, which ran through to Bolsover Street. Here we see the hospital preparing for war, with Matron Nellie Wood supervising the filling of sandbags by her nurses, who have rolled up their sleeves and are getting on with the job. This was the Bolsover Street entrance, with Great Portland Street station and Holy Trinity church in the background.

Great Titchfield Street from Langham Street, *c.* 1910. A memory of the days when Great Titchfield Street had a traditional street market. The road was also filled with useful domestic stores for the local populace, but although a few of these remain, there are mostly restaurants and shops associated with the garment industry here now.

Mrs J. Colby's shop, 37 Great Titchfield Street, *c.* 1905. This was one of the local stores, where a fine array of fish, game and poultry had been displayed to tempt the passer by. This was another postcard advertisement and was sent to one of the grand houses of Wimpole Street. Its survival suggests that the addressee was attracted to the service provided and therefore kept it.

MARSHALL'S SCHOOL OF COOKERY, 32, Mortimer St., London, W.1

VIEW OF CLASS ROOM

Marshall's School of Cookery, 32 Mortimer Street, 1922. This is another advertising postcard, this one giving details of 'an entire dinner lesson' which could be obtained at the private cookery school for 12/6d. The kitchen equipment was probably the last word in modernity in 1922, but the hard wooden benches for the would-be chefs, left, were hardly designed for comfort. There are modern offices at this address now.

Goodge Street, c. 1908. Mortimer Street runs eastward and becomes Goodge Street having passed the Middlesex Hospital. Goodge Street was for the most part in the borough of St Pancras (now Camden), but this section by Charlotte Place was Marylebone territory, with R. Winter's Drapery Market taking up most of the shops. These have since been split up into individual businesses.

Upper Marylebone Street, W

Upper Marylebone Street (New Cavendish Street) from Great Titchfield Street, 1910. This was the old name for the eastern portion of New Cavendish Street, which runs up to the borough boundary at Cleveland Street. The scene is a typically Edwardian one, with locals going about their business, including a lady who needed to be careful with her long skirt on the muddy roadway. The flats on the right were quite new and stand to this day, as does the Ship pub on the Saville Street (Hanson Street) corner; but Joseph Lovick's fried fish shop, which was sandwiched between them, has long gone. The sooty terraces to the left are also a distant memory, but there were useful stores there for the local populace, including a laundry, chemist and newsagent. Henry Oyler's garage was also here at, delightfully, number $44\frac{1}{2}$. The garage later became the Ogle Motor Co., (see page 62). The further terrace by Charlton Street (now also part of Hanson Street), was replaced by buildings for the London Polytechnic, now part of the University of Westminster. The photograph was contemporary with one of the great crime sensations of 1910, when Crippen, the murderer and his mistress Ethel le Neve were captured with the aid of wireless telegraphy as they fled across the Atlantic aboard the steamship *Montrose*. The newspapers were full of it all, as we may see here with newspaper placards proclaiming 'A surprise for Dr Crippen', while *The Star* offers 'A chat with Crippen'.

Six

Regent's Park
and St John's Wood

NDON. Regents Park. No. 1141.

Although much of Marylebone is urban in aspect, it also contains leafy St John's Wood and one of London's great royal parks, Regent's Park. Regent's Park was created from land which, before the seventeenth century, formed part of the great forest of Middlesex. By 1650, some 16,000 trees had been felled and for the next 150 years the land was used for agriculture. The development of the park as we know it stems from the early nineteenth century, when architect John Nash submitted plans for 'Marylebone Park', a private estate of villas and terraces set in picturesque parkland. Although much altered, the plans came to fruition and the first of the houses in Park Crescent were built in 1812. The celebrated terraces which border the park were constructed from the 1820s and survive today in sparkling condition, their cream stucco facades providing an unequalled display of Regency domestic architecture. The first part of the park opened to the public in 1836, from which time its popularity with Londoners was assured, with its flower gardens, water features and the London Zoo. Marylebone Park was renamed Regent's Park in honour of the Prince Regent. The view is of the boating lake and shows Londoners during the 1920s enjoying a sunny day in the park, much as they do today.

The Conservatory, Royal Botanic Society's Gardens, Regent's Park, c. 1906. The Royal Botanic Society of London was incorporated in 1839 and leased land for its gardens within Regent's Park's Inner Circle. The gardens were a great attraction and the glass conservatory enclosed an area of 15,000 square feet. When the society's lease expired in 1931, the area was transformed into a great rose garden, with eventually, some 25,000 specimens growing here. The garden was named after Queen Mary, wife of the monarch, King George V. Another new amenity, the famous Open Air Theatre, was founded here in 1932.

The Broad Walk, Regent's Park, c. 1920. Off for a stroll along the Broad Walk, a grand promenade running from Park Square in the south to Prince Albert Road in the north.

The Leopard's Cages, London Zoo, Regent's Park, c. 1904. The Zoological Society of London's gardens in Regent's Park were opened in 1828 and were soon popular enough for similar establishments to appear in other parts of the world. The Zoological Society was founded in 1824 and pioneered the scientific study of animals. The 'Zoo', the name which became popular from the 1860s, remains an essential part of the tourist's agenda and a popular place for a young Londoner's day out. The Edwardian visitors in the photograph were hoping for a glimpse of some rather elusive leopards.

(4) MAPPIN TERRACES, ZOOLOGICAL GARDENS.

The Mappin Terraces, Zoological Gardens, c. 1916. The innovative Mappin Terraces were a pioneering example of zoo building, with an artificial landscape which allowed the visitor to see the animals at close hand as they roamed in a seemingly cage-free environment. This was, of course, in the days before safari parks became popular in this country.

The Llama Ride, London Zoo, *c.* 1908. The zoo provided the chance for what would now be called a 'hands-on' experience of the less ferocious animals and a gentle llama ride was ideal for the younger visitors. The more adventurous and those with a head for heights, would have opted for the elephant ride.

Regent's Canal, Regent's Park, *c.* 1920. The Regent's Canal was opened in 1820 and ran from the Grand Junction Canal at Paddington Basin to the Thames at Limehouse. Nowadays, it makes an attractive water feature as it curves around the northern part of Regent's Park and pleasure craft run between Little Venice, Maida Vale and the trendy Camden Lock. The narrow boat seen here is from a more commercial past and was owned by British Portland Cement of Harefield, Middlesex.

Park Crescent, c. 1906. John Nash adopted the earlier Portland Place as the northern part of his great Regent Street scheme and gave it a suitably spectacular climax with this glorious crescent, which was designed on such a grand scale that photography of it all from ground level is barely possible. By the Edwardian era, Park Crescent had acquired a rather cluttered look at balcony level, with striped awnings and some ambitious foliage, while the house on the right had had an extra top floor added. Park Crescent was damaged during the Second World War, but reconstruction during the 1960s returned the crescent to the clean-cut elegance of its original design.

The Diorama, Park Square, c. 1905. Nash's plan for a northern Park Crescent facing the southern one would have created a vast circus, but the builder most inconveniently suffered bankruptcy and it was never built. The replacement scheme, Park Square, was begun in 1823 and included this remarkable building which housed a mechanical optical show in which painted scenery was artfully lit and rotated to simulate movement and colourful atmospheric effects, to the wonderment of an audience of 200. This forerunner of the cinema closed in 1851 and the building was converted to the form we see it here, a Baptist chapel. It is now the home of the Prince's Trust.

York Terrace from Cornwall Terrace, *c.* 1903. This stucco-fronted confection was designed by Nash, built in 1822 and provided its residents with exquisite views over Regent's Park's lakes and gardens. The unusually ornate lamp post on the right stood in front of Cornwall Terrace and several examples of these still survive. Other lamp posts in Regent's Park are among the oldest in London and bear the Royal cyphers for George IV (1820/30) and William IV (1830/37).

Cornwall Terrace, *c.* 1905. The classical magnificence of Cornwall Terrace, the oldest of the Regent's Park Terraces. It was built in 1820 to the design of Decimus Burton and was named after the Duke of Cornwall, an earlier title of King George IV who had just acceded to the throne.

Lincolnshire Farm Dairy, Boston Street, Taunton Place, *c.* 1905. This popular local shop was run by Miss Annie Wilks and catered for the everyday needs of residents in the small streets between the Great Central Railway and Regent's Park. The shop provided milk and bread deliveries and a mixture of groceries in the window included the still familiar 'Camp Coffee'.

Blandford Square, *c.* 1906. Blandford Square still exists as an address, but its fashionable days ended with the construction of the railway and Marylebone station during the 1890s. Blandford Square lost many of its houses at that time and left the survivors uncomfortably close to the railway's smoky cutting. Number 8 was still standing in 1906 and was home to this group of young Scotsmen who were working in London at that time. The last of the old houses were demolished in 1968 to be replaced by modern housing. The novelist George Eliot lived in the square from 1860/5.

Lord's, c. 1903. St John's Wood is home to Lord's, one of the world's greatest sporting venues, whose origins stretch back to 1787, when Thomas Lord secured a ground for the Marylebone Cricket Club in what is now Dorset Square. The club moved to North Bank, Regent's Park in 1811, but was displaced from there by the building of the Regent's Canal. A move to the present ground followed, with the first cricket match taking place there on 22 June 1814. The view is of a typically fashionable gathering during the University match between Oxford and Cambridge, when a sunny day has brought out the white parasols of the ladies to contrast with the formal wear of the gentlemen as they parade by Lord's Hotel (The Tavern) during an interval in play.

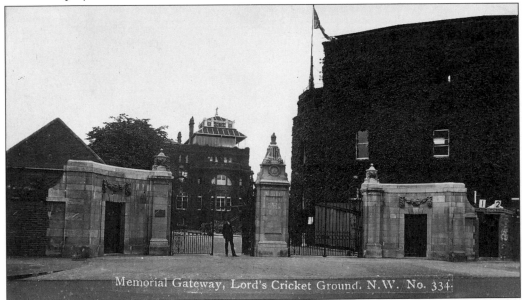

Memorial Gateway, Lord's Cricket Ground. N.W. No. 334.

The Grace Gates, Lord's, c. 1923. Cricketing legend Dr W.G. Grace, arguably the most famous exponent of the game, was suitably honoured by the erection of these gates at the headquarters of cricket in 1922. The central pillar bears the inscription: 'To the Memory of William Gilbert Grace, the Great Cricketer (1848-1915). These gates were erected by the MCC and other friends and admirers'.

St John's Wood Church, 1914. Now the parish church of St John's Wood, this stylish building was constructed in 1813 to the design of Thomas Hardwick as a chapel of ease to Marylebone church. The extensive burial ground at the back has been made into St John's Wood Church Grounds, an attractively leafy public garden.

Cochrane Street, 24 April 1908. St John's Wood experienced winter in the middle of spring on this icy Easter weekend, when freak snowfalls across southern England produced conditions more appropriate to Christmas. The effect in Cochrane Street was briefly picturesque, before it degenerated into the usual London slush. With the exception of one house, Cochrane Street has been entirely rebuilt during the present century and it is now a street of flats. The entrance to St John's Wood Church Grounds can be seen, centre.

Henry Street (Allitsen Road) from Charlbert Street, *c.* 1906. Even the more senior residents will be hard pressed to recognise this scene, for not only has the street name changed, but the entire character of the street has altered. To the left, the long shopping parade has given way to the flats of Cotman, Calderon and Ramsay Houses, part of the Townshend Estate, while on the right, the houses and shops by Eamont Street and beyond have all been rebuilt and the street lined with trees. Only the former school on the Charlbert Street corner, right, still stands together with the drinking fountain dated 1861. The street was renamed Allitsen Road during the 1930s; the name coming from Frances Allitsen, a songwriter popular around the turn of the century.

Henry Street (Allitsen Road), c. 1905. There were new flats to let, left, to contrast with some squalid properties opposite which were surviving remnants of a poor nineteenth-century district called Portland Town. These were about to be replaced by the smart flats of Park Mansions, but the next corner by Upper William Street (Bridgeman Street) would have to wait until 1940 for a new block of flats, Henry House, and a rebuilt Crown pub.

Townshend Road from Henry Street (Allitsen Road), c. 1908. With everyone in their Sunday best and every seat taken, a pair of well-laden horse-brakes prepares to depart from the New Inn for a jolly summer's day out. Horse-brakes like these were hired for the day and provided the Victorian and Edwardian equivalents of a motor coach excursion. The background reveals some more of dingy old Portland Town, with some grimy shops leading to Townshend Cottages and at the far right, St John's Wood Terrace. Nowadays, the New Inn stands alone on its corner overlooked by the six-storey flats of Cruikshank House. The cast iron bollard in the foreground was inscribed 'St Mary Le Bone 1828'. Although this one has gone, others have survived locally.

High Street (St John's Wood High Street), *c.* 1908. The street was originally called Portland Town Road before becoming 'High Street' and then 'St John's Wood High Street' in 1938. The twentieth century saw a considerable smartening up of this district, with old Portland Town giving way to affluent St John's Wood. These new shops, with some splendidly windowed accommodation above, arrived in 1903, while an empty site to the left awaited an extension of the shopping parade. The impressive Hanover House, a block of mansion flats, also of 1903 vintage, is on the right.

Circus Road from Eaton Terrace (Kingsmill Terrace), *c.* 1906. The name recalls a grand housing scheme of 1803 for a circular ring of houses, one mile in diameter, which, unfortunately, never materialised. The Princess Royal pub, right, has been rebuilt, together with the three shops of Thomas Bent, draper. The row of shops, left, now has a modern counterpart.

Acacia Gardens, *c.* 1905. A classical villa in a sylvan setting; this was the popular image of nineteenth century St John's Wood, which in part still survives. The twentieth century has dealt rather less kindly with Acacia Gardens, however, and there are modern town houses and a concrete road here now. St John's Wood Underground station was built close by in 1939.

Queen's Terrace, *c.* 1906. Only the far end of the nineteenth-century shopping parade has survived; the first building in it now being the Knights of St John Tavern (now closed), whose rooftop onion domes can be seen in the distance. The rest of the terrace has been replaced with a long row of flats whose name, Jubilee Buildings, recalls the Royal celebrations of the year they were built, 1935. The houses on the left have been replaced with Bartonway, another development of flats.

Nugent Terrace from Abercorn Place, *c.* 1905. This charming little Victorian shopping street has retained a village atmosphere and most of its buildings, apart from number 1, right, which has been rebuilt. The zig-zag skyline is of houses in Alma Square.

Blenheim Terrace from Abbey Road, *c.* 1925. Smart shops and restaurants now flourish in this well-preserved street in the northern part of St. John's Wood. Abbey Road post office was once a part of Storey & Son's grocery shop, left, but the post office can now be found on the opposite side of the road at number 14. The Durham Arms, centre, has been prettified and given a new name, the Drum and Monkey.

Alma Square, *c*. 1906. St John's Wood was much less built up than southern Marylebone, and there are less examples of that urban phenomenon, the garden square. Alma Square is quite unusual in its layout, with the gardens situated behind two of it's sides rather than in front, as is more usual. There are numerous 'Alma' street names in London; the name comes from a battle which took place during the Crimean War in 1854.

Loudoun Road, *c*. 1906. A customer fills his jug from the churn on the dairyman's cart, while children stand by in the sunshine of an Edwardian summer. This peaceful way of life has gone forever, and it would not be wise to stand in the middle of the road nowadays. Loudoun Road has retained many of it's fine old houses, but with many more modern ones mixed in.

Eyre Arms Riding School, 3 Finchley Road, *c.* 1905. David Hannay's riding school adjoined the Eyre Arms, a popular pub and hotel, which with Wellington Hall, its assembly rooms, was an ideal place for an evening's entertainment. The riding school provided a useful service at a time when horses still dominated the roads, and it was as well to learn the skills of horsemanship. David Hannay's business also involved the buying, selling, and hiring of horses as well as breaking them in. He also, no doubt, received a good income from the mass of advertisements which covered his walls, although the residents of the genteel villas, right, may not have been impressed by such an eyesore. Eyre Court, a massive complex of flats dating from 1930, now covers the sites of everything seen here.